B-N.

COLLINS BRIDGE
FOR BEGINNERS
DEFENCE
ZIA MAHMOOD

COLLINS BRIDGE
FOR BEGINNERS
DEFENCE

ZIA MAHMOOD

Foreword by Omar Sharif

CollinsWillow

An Imprint of HarperCollins*Publishers*

To L.B.

First published in 1990 as
Breakthrough Bridge: Defence for Beginners
by Virgin Books, UK

Revised edition published in 1994 by
Collins Willow
an imprint of HarperCollins*Publishers*, London

**A CIP catalogue record for this book
is available from the British Library**

ISBN 0 00 218469 9

Set in Palatino
by Wearset, Boldon, Tyne and Wear

Printed and bound in Great Britain by
The Guernsey Press Co. Ltd, Guernsey, Channel Islands

Contents

Foreword

I think it was just before filming *Lawrence of Arabia* that I first discovered that 'finesse' didn't necessarily mean choosing the correct vintage of Dom Perignon. It was a discovery that changed my life, as this introduction to the game of bridge, which developed initially as a method of combating the frequent boredom of filmmaking, changed to a passion and an involvement that are stronger today than ever. It would be difficult to count the hours of pleasure I have received from bridge, surely the most fascinating of games ever invented, and I hope that you too can derive the same joy after this introduction to the game.

Zia has long been a friend of mine and he is rated by many as the No 1 player in the world. In my opinion, however, his contribution has been much more than expertise because of the charisma and sense of fun that he brings with him to the game. He is the living proof that bridge is not a boring game for boring people but an exciting game that mixes all the most vital human qualities and emotions.

In the *Bridge for Beginners* series, Zia has combined his expertise and sense of humour with the talents of the internationally known teacher and author Audrey Grant to bring an introduction to the game that is essential for all beginners.

For once, you can learn the secrets of the game presented in a simple yet entertaining manner that is as much fun to read as to play. For once, you can actually listen to an expert as he talks you through his thoughts on every basic step and situation. Finally, once you have read this book, I hope you will take up the game of bridge as I once did, because I already know that its lure is irresistible once felt, its addiction heady and exciting, and I would like to share this knowledge.

Omar Sharif

CHAPTER 1

Introduction

It is generally accepted that contract bridge started in about 1925 when Harold Sterling Vanderbilt was cruising the Caribbean on the SS Finland. He picked up a pack of cards, shuffled them, and said 'Gentlemen, let me show you a new game. It may interest you.'

Bridge is said to be the Rolls-Royce of card games, and for good reason. It can be as comfortable as your favourite pair of shoes, and yet at the same time it can excite you as much after you have played for years as when you first experienced the game. Bridge can be a quiet source of pleasure when you play in familiar surroundings with friends you have known all your life, or a tool which introduces you to new people in new places. Tennis star Martina Navratilova once said that bridge meant a lot to her in her travels: 'No matter where I go,' she said, 'I can always make new friends at the bridge table'. Omar Sharif is said to have given up acting, horses and women for the game. For others, bridge is a great social activity. It is difficult to believe that bridge is good for us; to believe that something that brings so much joy is not immoral, against the law or bad for our health. If you are not yet familiar with the game, what have you been waiting for? If you have played for years, it's time to introduce you to some of the secrets of the experts, taught, we hope, with a mixture of fun and simplicity.

Getting started

All you need are three other people and a *pack* of cards. If you have a card table, four chairs and a pencil and paper to keep score, so much the better. Already you are as well-equipped as a world champion!

Bridge is a partnership game. Although you can play with a regular partner, it is common to *cut* for partners. To do this, take the cards and spread them face down on the table. Each player selects a card and turns it up. The cards are ranked as usual in this order: Ace (highest), King, Queen, Jack, 10, 9, 8, 7, 6, 5, 4, 3, 2 (lowest). The players choosing the two higher-ranking cards play together and those picking the two lower-ranking cards are partners. If the four cards turned over were an ace, a king, a jack and a 3, the players choosing the ace and king would play together and the players turning over the jack and 3 would be partners.

What if two players pick the same ranked card? Let's consider a most unusual case where all four players pick aces. It looks as if there is a four-way tie, but there is a method of breaking such a tie. The *suits* are ranked in alphabetical order with the clubs (♣) being the lowest ranked suit, then diamonds (♦), hearts (♥) and, at the top, the highest ranking suit, spades (♠). In the situation mentioned above, then, the players with the ace of spades (♠A) and ace of hearts (♥A) would play against the players holding the ace of diamonds (♦A) and ace of clubs (♣A).

The partners sit opposite one another. Bridge writers refer to the players not by name but by direction: North, East, South and West. Here, then, are the four players sitting round the table:

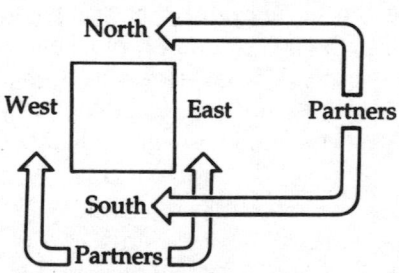

Introducing the play

Once everyone is sitting down and ready to play, the player who chose the highest card deals. The jokers are not used, so a bridge pack consists of 52 cards. Starting with the player on his left, the dealer deals one card at a time to each player, proceeding clockwise around the table, until the pack is exhausted and each player has 13 cards. If, during the deal, a card is accidentally turned face up, the deal must be restarted – the pack must be shuffled and cut, and the dealer tries again! Each player picks up his *hand* and sorts it into suits. It is easier to see your hand if you separate the black and red suits. Here is a sorted bridge hand:

In a book or newspaper, the above bridge hand is usually written out in the ranking order of the suits, with spades first, then hearts, diamonds and clubs as follows:

♠ A J 3
♡ K 9 7 4
◇ Q 8 2
♣ J 10 5

The objective during the play of the hand is for your partnership to try to take as many *tricks* as you can. A trick consists of four cards, one from each player, and the player contributing the highest card wins the trick for his side. The player who wins each trick *leads* the first card to the next trick face up on the table and the other three players play their cards, in turn, clockwise around the table. Everyone has to *follow suit* to the first card that is led, if they can. For example, let's suppose that West leads the king of spades. All the other players, in turn, have to follow suit by playing a spade, if they have one. Suppose North contributes the ace of spades, the highest card in the suit, East plays the 3 of spades and South plays the 2 of spades. North has won the trick for his side (North-South). Here is the trick:

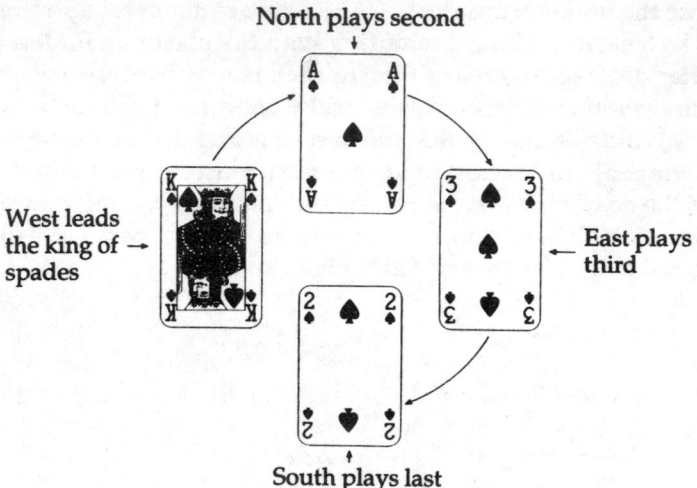

You can see that North plays second, West leads the king of spades, East plays third, and South plays last.

North collects the four cards and puts them in a stack face down in front of himself. Usually, one member of the partnership collects all the tricks won for his side. At the end of the hand, thirteen tricks will have been played and the table might look like this:

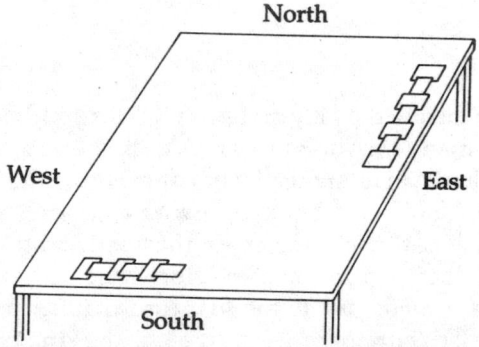

You can see that North-South took six tricks and East-West took seven. The game can be played in one of two ways: with a trump suit, or in no trumps. In no trumps, the highest card played in the suit led always wins the trick. If you cannot follow suit, you must play a card in another suit, but a card *discarded* in this way has no power to win the trick, even if it is higher-ranking than the card led. To take an unlikely example: West leads the two of clubs, on which North plays the ace of spades, East the ace of hearts and South the ace of diamonds. West is the winner of the trick, for his two was the highest – indeed the only – card played in the suit led. The winner of the trick, when playing in no trumps, is the person who played the highest card in the suit that was led.

The game can also be played in a *trump* suit where one suit becomes the most powerful suit for that hand. If you cannot follow suit you can play a trump and it will win the trick, provided a higher trump is not played on the same trick. For example, let's suppose that clubs have been designated as the trump suit. West leads the ◊A, North plays the ◊5, East plays the ◊3 and South plays the ♣2. The trick looks like this:

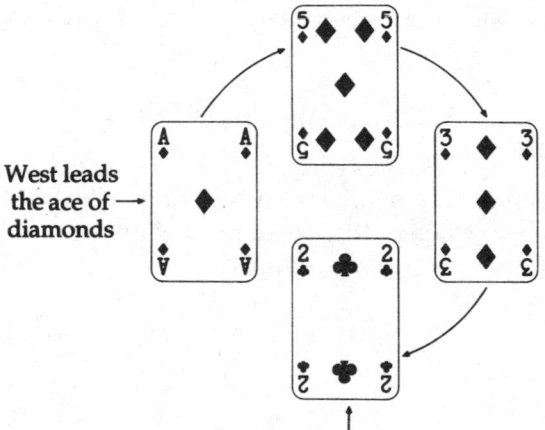

West leads the ace of diamonds →

↑
South wins the trick with the two of clubs (note that he must have no diamonds)

Because clubs are trumps, the small club wins the trick. South, however, can only play the ♣2 if he has no diamonds left in his hand. Otherwise, he must follow suit by playing a diamond on the trick. South does not have to play a trump if he has no diamonds. Instead, he can discard a heart or spade and let West win the trick with the ◊A. It is permitted to lead trumps. If the trump suit is led, the highest trump played wins the trick. Let's summarise all these points about playing the cards:

Summary of play of the hand

1 You and your partner work together to take as many tricks as you can.
2 When one player leads a card to a trick, all other players must follow suit if they can. If a player cannot follow suit, he plays a card from another suit.
3 The player who wins the trick leads to the next trick. Each player follows clockwise in turn.
4 In no trumps, the highest card of the suit led wins the trick.
5 When playing with a trump suit, if a player cannot follow suit he can choose to play a trump. If more than one trump is played to a trick, the highest trump played wins the trick. This is the only exception to the cardinal rule of trick taking which is that the highest card played in the suit led always wins the trick.

Introducing the bidding

In some card games, the trump suit is decided by turning up a card, sometimes from another pack. In bridge, each player gets an opportunity to suggest that the longest suit in his hand be the trump suit. Suppose this is your hand:

♠ 3 2
♡ A K 7 5 2
◊ 7 3
♣ A K 7 3

Your longest suit is hearts and so you would suggest that hearts be trumps, by bidding hearts. Now let's look at your partner's hand:

♠ A 8 6 5 4
♡ 6
◊ 9 6 2
♣ Q J 8 6

The longest suit in your partner's hand is spades, so that would be his first choice, or bid. The bidding is simply a conversation that you have with your partner to reach a consensus about the trump suit. One drawback is that you have to reach this decision without seeing your partner's hand. That seems fair, doesn't it? Can you imagine how colourless the game would be if you could look at one another's hands? Another limitation is that you cannot mention the actual cards that you hold in a suit or the number of cards that you hold in each suit. It would take away the challenge if you could say to your partner that you have the ace, king, 7, 5 and 2 of hearts or that you have a four-card club suit headed by the ace and king.

Instead, the type of conversation you and your partner could have with the above hands would, possibly, go something like this:

You: I like hearts better than any other suit.
Partner: I like spades best; I don't have many hearts.
You: I don't like spades very much but what do you think about clubs?
Partner: I don't mind clubs.
You: So let's agree to choose clubs as our trump suit.
Partner: Seems reasonable.

This is the concept of bidding. It really is this simple, except for a very small catch we will come to shortly. You and your partner are having a conversation to tell each other as much as possible about your hands. How did you and your partner do in the above discussion? You found your longest combined suit, which is the idea of bidding. In either hearts or spades, on these hands, you have only seven combined cards in the suit. In clubs you and your partner have an eight-card *fit*, which means you have eight cards in the suit between the two hands. No matter how far you go in bridge, bidding should never be more complicated than the concept of a conversation between two friends.

The partnership, through the bidding, tries to uncover the suit in which it holds the most cards – the suit that would make the best trump suit. A good trump suit is usually one containing eight or more cards between the two hands. Since there are thirteen cards in a suit, if your side has eight, the opponents have only five cards and you hold the clear majority of the suit. If you can make your longest combined suit the trump suit, you will be able to use your small trump cards to help win tricks whenever you cannot follow suit, since they will then have more value than even the ace in a suit that is not trumps.

Now, about that catch! Let's take another look at the bidding. When you play a game of bridge, you are expected to use only the language and the vocabulary of the game. You cannot actually say 'I like hearts, how about you?' The good news, however, is that the bridge language is spoken world-wide and the vocabulary consists of only a handful of words: the numbers from one to seven; the names of the suits – clubs, diamonds, hearts and spades – or no trumps; and the words *pass* or *no bid*. These few simple words are all you need to describe your hand.

A bid is a combination of a number and a denomination (a suit or no trumps). A bid, for example, would be one heart (1♡), three spades (3♠), six no trumps (6NT) or seven clubs (7♣). You can envisage that, if you say one heart (1♡), it means you like hearts. The number refers to the number of tricks you are expected to take if you win the bid. One heart, however, does not refer to taking only one trick with hearts as trumps. Six tricks, referred to as your *book*, must be added to the number of the bid. If you say 'one heart', you and your partner would have to take seven (6 + 1 = 7) tricks if your bid for the trump suit is accepted. The idea behind this assumed book of six tricks in addition to the number that you actually bid is that you must commit yourselves to taking the majority of the thirteen tricks available if you want your suit to be the trump suit.

Bridge bidding is like an auction. The players try to outbid each other for the privilege of naming the trump suit. There is no auctioneer, however. Instead there is an agreed-upon, orderly way of conducting the bidding.

The dealer gets the first opportunity to open the bidding by suggesting a denomination (a trump suit or no trumps). If he does not want to commit his side to trying to take at least seven tricks – the minimum requirement for opening the bidding – he can say 'Pass' or 'No bid'. Each player, clockwise in turn, then gets a chance to make a bid or to pass. The auction continues round the table until a bid is followed by three passes, meaning that everyone is in agreement with the last bid, and no one wants to bid any further.

What if one player bids 1♠ and the next player wants to bid 1◇? Which bid is higher? There is an automatic tie-breaker built into the language of bridge. The suits are ranked, remember, in ascending alphabetical order (clubs, diamonds, hearts, spades). No trumps is considered to rank the highest of all, higher than spades. Since diamonds are lower-ranking than spades, a 1♠ bid outranks a 1◇ bid. If the next player wants to suggest diamonds as the trump suit, he will have to commit his side to taking more tricks by raising the level and bidding 2◇. On the other hand, if the next player wants to suggest no trumps, he can bid 1NT, since that outranks the 1♠ bid.

We can think of the possible bids as a series of steps leading from one level to the next as illustrated below:

The bidding steps

$$7♣\ 7◇\ 7♡\ 7♠\ 7NT$$
$$6♣\ 6◇\ 6♡\ 6♠\ 6NT$$
$$5♣\ 5◇\ 5♡\ 5♠\ 5NT$$
$$4♣\ 4◇\ 4♡\ 4♠\ 4NT$$
$$3♣\ 3◇\ 3♡\ 3♠\ 3NT$$
$$2♣\ 2◇\ 2♡\ 2♠\ 2NT$$
$$1♣\ 1◇\ 1♡\ 1♠\ 1NT$$

Each bid must be further up or further to the right on the bidding steps than the preceding bid. If a player starts the bidding at the one level (1♣, 1◇, 1♡, 1♠ or 1NT), contracting to take seven tricks, another player can make a bid in a higher-ranking denomination at the one level or must climb to the two level, contracting to take eight tricks, if he wants to make a bid in a lower-ranking denomination. If a player does not want to bid any higher, he will pass.

Hearts and spades are referred to as the *major* suits and, when you look at the bidding steps, you can see they are higher-ranking than clubs and diamonds which are referred to as the *minor* suits.

After there are three passes, the last bid determines the trump suit and the number of tricks that the side naming this trump suit must take to be successful. The final bid becomes the *contract*. Let's look at our two hands to see how they would be bid using the language of bridge. We will assume that the opponents do not wish to compete for the contract and choose to pass throughout the auction.

You	*Partner*
♠ 3 2	♠ A 8 6 5 4
♡ A K 7 5 2	♡ 6
◇ 7 3	◇ 9 6 2
♣ A K 7 3	♣ Q J 8 6

You:	*One heart.*	(I like hearts and am contracting to take seven tricks with hearts as trumps.)
Partner:	*One spade.*	(I would prefer spades as trumps. I can keep the bidding at the one level since spades rank higher than hearts.)
You	*Two clubs.*	(You don't seem to like my hearts. How about clubs? I have to move to the two level to show my second suit since clubs are lower-ranking than spades.)
Partner:	*Pass*	(I like clubs much better than hearts and they should make a satisfactory trump suit. I do not want to go any higher up the bidding steps since we are already contracting to take eight tricks.)

Let's suppose you are sitting in the South position and your partner is North. This is the way the above auction would normally be written down, showing your opponents' passes as well as your bids:

South	*West*	*North*	*East*
1♡	Pass	1♠	Pass
2♣	Pass	Pass	Pass

West, North and East all have to say pass after the 2♣ bid in order to end the auction. North-South are said to have won the bid and the *final contract* is 2♣. What happens next?

Introducing the roles of each side

After the bidding is completed, one partnership has been successful in naming the trump suit and, in the process, has arrived at a contract, which is a commitment to take a certain number of tricks. In the example above, North-South arrived at a contract of 2♣ and, in doing so, committed to take eight tricks with clubs as trumps. If they take at least eight tricks with clubs as trump, they make their contract. If they are not successful in collecting eight tricks, then East-West defeat the contract. East-West are said to be the *defence* and they are trying to prevent North-South from taking enough tricks to fulfil the contract.

One player from the side who wins the contract is called the *declarer* and that player is going to play both his and his partner's hands. The other hand is referred to as the *dummy*. Which player is the declarer and which player is the dummy? The player who first mentioned the suit that ended up being the trump suit (or whoever bid no trumps first in a no trump contract is the declarer and his partner becomes the dummy. In the auction above, South is the declarer since he was the first to mention the club suit and his partner, North, is the dummy. The player to the left of the declarer makes the opening lead. In this case, it would be West and he would choose a card and place it on the table. North's hand, the dummy, is then placed face up on the table. The trump suit is put on dummy's right – the declarer's left. Suppose the opening lead is the ◊K. After the dummy is put down, the cards on the table might look like this:

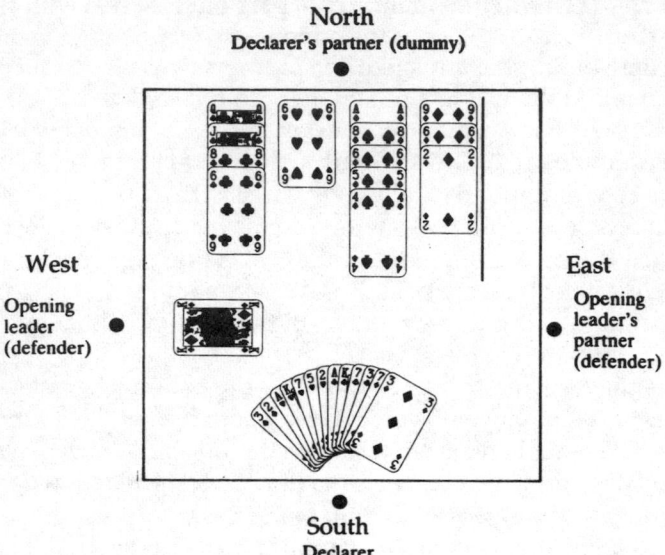

North
Declarer's partner (dummy)

West
Opening leader (defender)

East
Opening leader's partner (defender)

South
Declarer

In order to discuss the play from the declarer's viewpoint, the hand is usually illustrated as follows:

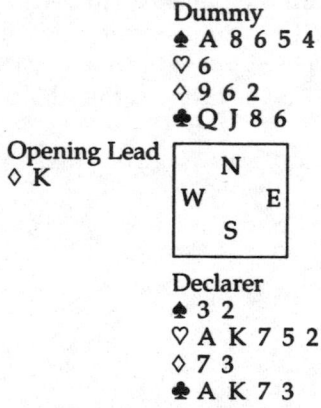

Dummy
♠ A 8 6 5 4
♡ 6
♦ 9 6 2
♣ Q J 8 6

Opening Lead
♦ K

```
    N
W      E
    S
```

Declarer
♠ 3 2
♡ A K 7 5 2
♦ 7 3
♣ A K 7 3

The *defenders* (East-West) can take the first two diamond tricks but you can trump the third round of diamonds with one of your clubs. This is one of the advantages of playing this hand with clubs as the trump suit. It prevents the opponents from taking too many tricks with their diamond suit.

Introducing the scoring

In the above hand, when you take the eight tricks to which you committed yourself in the auction, you are awarded a certain number of *points* for fulfilling the contract. The exact details of the scoring are contained in the appendix on p. 171. All that is important for now is that you have a general idea of how the game is scored. The partnership which earns the higher number of points from all the hands that are played wins the game. Points can be scored in three ways:

- If you *make* (fulfil) your contract, you are given a trick score for each trick you take beyond your book of six tricks.
- If you defeat the opponents' contract, by preventing them from taking the number of tricks to which they committed themselves, you gain points for each trick by which you defeat their contract. In effect, your opponents suffer a penalty when they *go down* (are defeated) in their contract.
- Points are awarded for reaching and making certain bonus level contracts.

Summary

The four players form two partnerships, with the partners sitting opposite each other across the table.

After the cards have been dealt out, the players, in clockwise rotation starting with the dealer, have an opportunity to suggest the denomination (trump suit or no trumps) in which they would like to play the hand.

Each bid must be higher on the bidding steps than the previous bid. If a player does not want to bid, he says pass or no bid.

The side willing to commit itself to the greater number of tricks for the privilege of naming the denomination wins the auction.

The last bid becomes the final contract.

Defence

The player who first suggested the denomination of the final contract becomes the declarer and his partner becomes the dummy.

The defender to the left of the declarer leads to the first trick and then the dummy's hand is placed face up on the table.

The declarer tries to take the number of tricks his side committed itself to in bidding the final contract. He plays the cards from both the dummy and his own hand on each trick.

The defenders try to take enough tricks to defeat the contract.

With this introduction, you are ready to play.

CHAPTER 2

General Principles

Investing in a new sport can be costly. When you decide to take up bridge all the equipment you need is a pack of cards, a table, and four people. Already you are as well-prepared as a world champion.

Defence has been labelled the most difficult part of the game of bridge. That is certainly true, but it is as intriguing and exciting as it is difficult. You defend contracts twice as often as you end up being *declarer* since, when your side is playing the contract, you are the *dummy* half the time, whereas a defender is involved in every hand and has to be constantly alert.

Becoming a good *defender*, therefore, can double your effectiveness at the bridge table. In addition, when you take the opportunity to think about the defence of a hand, the game becomes much more interesting. Rather than waiting for those occasions when you are declarer, you find yourself looking forward to every hand.

The defenders are interested in preventing the declarer from making his contract. They work as a team, but the catch is, unlike the declarer, they don't have the benefit of being able to see each other's cards. This is quite a test because they are dealing with the unknown. In the game of bridge, your relationship with your partner is as important as luck and skill, and this is constantly tested when you have to use your imagination and work as a team to defeat the declarer's contract. In this book, we will let you in on some of the secrets of the experts and show you how they make magic from their cards when they are defending. In this book, the declarer will always be in the South position and the dummy in the North position. You will sometimes be West, and sometimes East.

Making a plan

Most bridge books traditionally start teaching defence by concentrating on rules for making the opening lead. A typical example would be for a beginner to be shown a hand like the following and asked what he would lead against a no-trump contract:

♠ A K
♡ 8 4
◊ Q J 10 6 5
♣ 6 5 3 2

The most crucial point of the defence, however, and the concept that will make you more effective, is to understand that it is necessary to look at the big picture before you are ever able to select an opening lead. What no-trump contract are you defending against? 1NT, 3NT or 6NT?

The defenders, in the same manner as the declarer, get their best results through making a plan. Always take a moment to think about how you are going to defeat the contract before playing a card. The letters S T O P can be used to help you remember the steps to go through in defence as in declarer play. **STOP** stands for:

S – stop to consider your goal
T – tally your winners
O – organize your plan
P – put your plan into operation

Defence has two parts, so you will sometimes have to STOP twice. First, before the opening lead when all you have to go on is the bidding and your hand; then, after the dummy goes down and you have more information.

Stop to consider your goal

The first step when defending is to consider your goal. How many tricks do you and your partner need to defeat the contract? This might seem an elementary point and yet, whether you are a world champion or a beginner, the process is the same. If the opponents are playing in a contract of 3NT, you need five tricks to defeat the contract. If they are playing in 6NT, you need only two tricks. The goal affects each card played by the partnership, starting with the opening lead.

Tally your winners

After you have considered the partnership's goal, the next step is to see how close you are to getting there. Tally your winners. A *winner*, or a *sure trick*, is a trick you can take without giving up the lead to the declarer. For example, look at the following hand and consider how many winners you have:

♠ 10 7 2
♡ A 8 6 5 4
♢ K Q
♣ 8 3 2

You have one winner, the ♡A. Although there is good potential for an extra trick in the diamond suit, there is no sure trick. If declarer has the ♢A, you would have to give up the lead before you could take a trick in the diamond suit. Now, consider this hand:

♠ 7 4
♡ Q 9 6 5 4
♢ A K Q
♣ A 5 3

Here, you have four sure tricks: the ♢A, ♢K, ♢Q and ♣A. One final example:

♠ 3
♡ J 8 4 3 2
♢ K J 10
♣ A Q 4 3

There is only one winner. You have lots of potential for taking more tricks, but the only trick you can take for sure is the ♣A.

There is an interesting difference between counting sure tricks when you are the declarer and counting them when you are a defender. Take a look at this layout of cards from the declarer's point of view:

Dummy
♡ Q 10 4

	N	
W		E
	S	

Declarer
♡ A K 2

When you are the declarer, you can see that there are three sure tricks in the heart suit. Now let's look at a similar holding from the defender's point of view:

You
◊ Q 10 4

	N	
W		E
	S	

Partner
◊ A K 2

Your ◊Q is a winner against a no-trump contract (and against a suit contract, unless the declarer is void), but you are unlikely to be sure that it is a winner since you cannot see your partner's cards.

A defender, therefore, must be more flexible than a declarer when it comes to counting winners. You have to be prepared to recognize the potential for tricks by making assumptions about your partner's hand. As we shall see, the bidding and any cards that have already been played will often give you clues as to where your side's winners lie.

Organize your plan

Having considered your goal and counted your sure tricks, you can see how close you are to reaching your objective. You now look at the options available to get you to your target. Let's bring back our first hand:

♠ A K
♡ 8 4
◊ Q J 10 6 5
♣ 6 5 3 2

Let's first suppose you are defending against a contract of 6NT. The first step of the plan tells you that your goal is to take two tricks in order to defeat the contract. The second step tells you that you have two winners. When you come to the third step, you don't need to think of any ways of developing additional tricks, since you already have enough winners to defeat the contract. You can move on to putting your plan into action.

Suppose, however, that you are defending against a contract of 3NT. Now you need five tricks to defeat the contract but have only two sure winners. At the third step of your plan, you are going to have to look for ways to develop the extra tricks you need. After examining the options, you will have to organize them to give your side the best chance of defeating the contract.

Your focus would shift from the spade suit to the diamond suit, since it appears to have the potential to develop the extra tricks you need. If your partner had bid hearts or clubs during the auction, you would consider the option of leading his suit to try and establish the winners you need. With more than one choice, you will have to decide which approach gives you the best chance of defeating the contract. Sometimes, you may even be able to combine your chances. The remaining chapters in this book will focus on the options the defenders have for developing the additional winners they need.

Put your plan into operation

Only after you have gone through the first three steps of your plan are you ready to choose a card to play. Even though you have decided on the suit you are going to play, there may be a consideration as to which card you should play in the suit. By choosing the card carefully, you may be able to give information to your partner.

In our example hand above, having decided that you should

lead a diamond against a contract of 3NT, most players would lead the ◇Q, top of a *sequence*. As we shall see in later chapters, there are technical reasons for selecting a specific card from your holding in a suit.

You do not simply make a plan before choosing the opening lead. Both partners must be formulating a plan on every hand. Often, your plan will have to change as you acquire additional information.

For example, suppose your partner has led the ♣5 against a contract of 3NT and, after seeing the dummy, you (East) have to choose what to do on the following hand:

Contract: 3NT

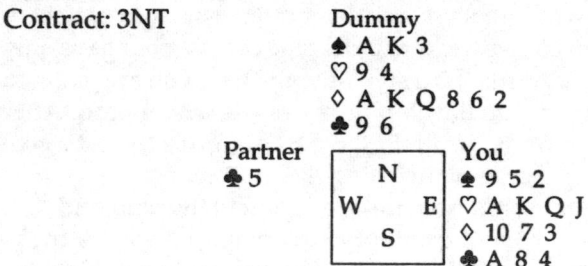

```
                    Dummy
                    ♠ A K 3
                    ♡ 9 4
                    ◇ A K Q 8 6 2
                    ♣ 9 6
        Partner                   You
        ♣ 5      ┌─────────┐      ♠ 9 5 2
                 │    N    │      ♡ A K Q J
                 │ W     E │      ◇ 10 7 3
                 │    S    │      ♣ A 8 4
                 └─────────┘
```

Stop to consider your goal
You are defending against a contract of 3NT and so you need to take five tricks. That is your goal.

Tally your winners
A winner is a trick you can take without giving up the lead to the opponents. Look at the cards you hold in each suit and count the sure tricks:

Spades:　　　0 winners
Hearts　　　　4 winners
Diamonds:　　0 winners
Clubs:　　　　1 winner

The total is five sure tricks. This is enough to reach your goal.

Organize your plan

You have the option of winning the first trick with the ♣A or playing one of your other clubs. If you win the ♣A, you have the option of *returning your partner's suit,* by leading another club, or switching to a different suit. Since the first two steps of your plan have told you that you have enough sure tricks to defeat the contract, you do not have to look further.

Put your plan into operation

This hand is quite straightforward. Win the first trick with the ♣A and take your four heart tricks, defeating the contract. You can then lead another club and see if your partner has any more tricks for the defence.

Looking at the complete hand, you can see that doing anything else would be fatal:

Contract: 3NT

```
                    ♠ A K 3
                    ♡ 9 4
                    ◇ A K Q 8 6 2
                    ♣ 9 6
     ♠ Q 10 8 4    ┌─────────┐    ♠ 9 5 2
     ♡ 8 6 3 2     │    N    │    ♡ A K Q J
     ◇ 5           │ W     E │    ◇ 10 7 3
     ♣ Q 10 7 5    │    S    │    ♣ A 8 4
                   └─────────┘
                    ♠ J 7 6
                    ♡ 10 7 5
                    ◇ J 9 4
                    ♣ K J 3 2
```

If you did not win the first trick with the ♣A, the declarer would win the first trick and quickly scamper home, taking two spade tricks and six diamond tricks in addition to the first trick. The same thing would happen if, after winning the ♣A, you do anything except take your four heart tricks.

Let's change your hand slightly from the previous example:

Contract: 3NT

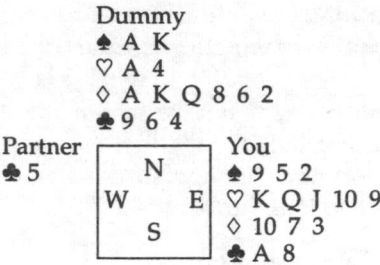

```
                    Dummy
                    ♠ A K
                    ♡ A 4
                    ◊ A K Q 8 6 2
                    ♣ 9 6 4
        Partner          You
        ♣ 5              ♠ 9 5 2
           N             ♡ K Q J 10 9
        W     E          ◊ 10 7 3
           S             ♣ A 8
```

Stop to consider your goal
You again need to take five tricks to defeat the contract.

Tally your winners
Look at your sure tricks in each suit:

Spades: 0 winners
Hearts: 0 winners
Diamonds: 0 winners
Clubs: 1 winner

Although you have a strong-looking heart suit, you do not have sure winners in that suit since you will have to *drive out* the dummy's ♡A first.

Organize your plan
Again you have a couple of options. You can win the ♣A and lead another club, returning your partner's suit. Alternatively, you can win the ♣A and lead a heart, planning to drive out the ♡A and establish four heart tricks, enough to defeat the contract if you can regain the lead. It is certainly not a good idea to let the declarer win the first club trick, since he will immediately be able to take two spade tricks, a heart trick and six diamond tricks to make the contract.

Should you switch to hearts or lead back a club? This is the type of situation you will often encounter when defending. It would help if you could see your partner's cards, but you cannot. You will have to try to visualize a holding in your partner's hand that would allow you to defeat the contract. If you switch to a heart, the declarer will be able to win the ♡A and take enough tricks to make the contract. Instead, you will have to hope that your partner has a good enough club suit to let the defence take the first five tricks.

Put your plan into operation
Having gone through your plan, you come down to your only option of winning the ♣A and leading back your remaining club. The rest is up to your partner. Let's take a look at the complete hand:

Contract: 3NT

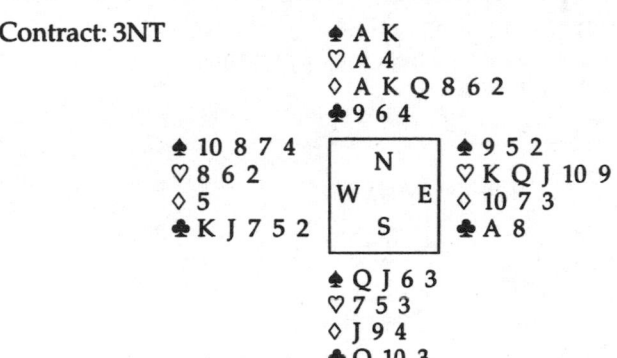

```
                      ♠ A K
                      ♡ A 4
                      ◊ A K Q 8 6 2
                      ♣ 9 6 4
   ♠ 10 8 7 4                        ♠ 9 5 2
   ♡ 8 6 2          ┌─────────┐      ♡ K Q J 10 9
   ◊ 5          W   │    N    │  E   ◊ 10 7 3
   ♣ K J 7 5 2      │    S    │      ♣ A 8
                    └─────────┘
                      ♠ Q J 6 3
                      ♡ 7 5 3
                      ◊ J 9 4
                      ♣ Q 10 3
```

As you can see, your club return traps the declarer's ♣Q and allows your partner to take four more club tricks to defeat the contract. By always making a plan first, you will find yourself making the right decisions in defence.

Summary

Before deciding what card to lead or what card to play on a particular trick, STOP to consider the total picture. What is your goal? How close are you to reaching it? Organize a plan: either take your winners if you have enough on your own to defeat the contract or develop a way of getting the extra tricks your partnership needs. Only after you have gone through the plan are you ready to put it into operation.

The defenders have more of a challenge because they cannot see each other's hands. They each have to keep very open minds when making their plan and must be ready to adjust as they see the cards played by their partner and the declarer.

Over Zia's shoulder

Now we are going to watch Zia in action to see how even a world-class player has to STOP to make a plan before deciding on what card to play in a specific suit. We are going to look over Zia's shoulder. Sometimes Zia will be in the position of making the opening lead and will be sitting West; at other times he will be sitting East and his partner will have made the opening lead.

In each example, we will give the auction first and then you can see how Zia endeavours to defeat the opponents.

Here's our first hand:

Hand 1 Dealer: South

North	East	South	West
			(Zia)
		1◇	Pass
1♡	Pass	2NT	Pass
6NT	Pass	Pass	Pass

(Zia)
♠ 9 6
♡ 10 9 8 6 2
◇ K 7 3
♣ K Q 10

```
      N
  W       E
      S
```

The very first hand and I find myself on lead against a slam. I hope the opponents aren't going to have such good hands all the time. Against no-trump contracts, I usually lead my longest suit, hoping to develop as many tricks as I can for our side. Before leading a card, however, I'm going to STOP and go through the steps of my plan. How are we going to defeat this slam contract?

Solution to Hand 1:

Contract: 6NT

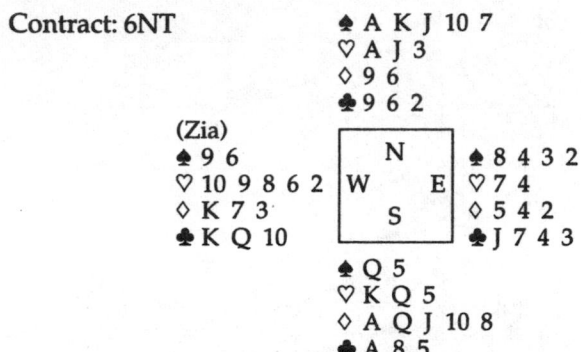

♠ A K J 10 7
♡ A J 3
◇ 9 6
♣ 9 6 2

(Zia)
♠ 9 6
♡ 10 9 8 6 2
◇ K 7 3
♣ K Q 10

♠ 8 4 3 2
♡ 7 4
◇ 5 4 2
♣ J 7 4 3

♠ Q 5
♡ K Q 5
◇ A Q J 10 8
♣ A 8 5

S Stop to consider the goal. We need two tricks to defeat 6NT.

T Tally the winners. We look to see how many sure tricks we have in each suit and can't find any. Not a good start for the defence. I always like to have a couple of aces to lead against a slam.

O Organize the plan. We won't get any tricks in spades or hearts unless my partner has a high card in one of the suits. Since the opponents have bid a slam, that is unlikely. I might get a trick with the ◇K, since the opponent on my right bid diamonds. I can also develop a trick by leading the ♣K to drive out the ♣A and establish my ♣Q. That looks like the best chance for two tricks.

P Put the plan into operation. I lead the ♣K and the declarer wins the ♣A. After he takes some spade tricks, he leads a diamond from the dummy and plays the ◇Q. I win the trick with the ◇K and quickly take the ♣Q to defeat the contract.

In fact, we can take three more tricks – the ♣Q, partner's ♣J and the thirteenth club in the East hand. Three down in a slam contract that would have been made had we not taken time to make a plan! If I had led a heart, instead of the ♣K, the declarer would have won the trick and played on the diamond suit. Although he would lose a trick to my ◇K, he would have the rest of the tricks no matter what I led back. I'll bet that my partner was happy to see us defeat the contract with his pathetic collection of cards!

Hand 2 Dealer: North

North	East (Zia)	South	West
1♣	Pass	1♡	Pass
4♡	Pass	Pass	Pass

```
                         Dummy
                         ♠ Q 3
                         ♡ K Q 7 5
                         ◊ Q 6
                         ♣ A K Q J 3
          Partner                    (Zia)
          ♠ 10       ┌─────────┐     ♠ A K 7
                     │    N    │     ♡ A 8 2
                     │ W     E │     ◊ 10 8 7 3 2
                     │    S    │     ♣ 10 8
                     └─────────┘
```

This time, they've only bid to a game contract. Let's try and keep our record intact by defeating this contract as well. Partner seems to have found a good lead since it looks as though I'm going to get two sure spade tricks. That won't be enough to defeat the contract, however, so I'd better STOP and make a plan.

Solution to Hand 2:

Contract: 4♡

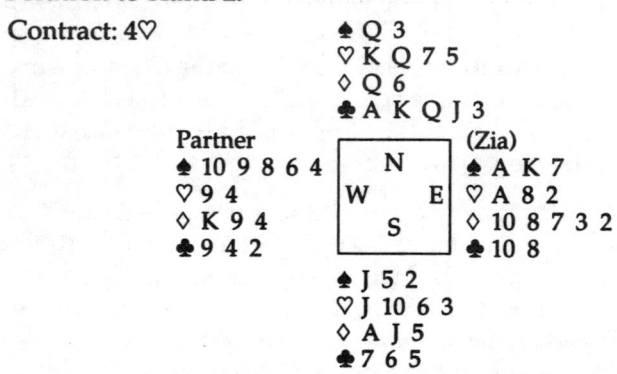

```
                         ♠ Q 3
                         ♡ K Q 7 5
                         ◊ Q 6
                         ♣ A K Q J 3
          Partner                    (Zia)
          ♠ 10 9 8 6 4 ┌─────────┐   ♠ A K 7
          ♡ 9 4        │    N    │   ♡ A 8 2
          ◊ K 9 4      │ W     E │   ◊ 10 8 7 3 2
          ♣ 9 4 2      │    S    │   ♣ 10 8
                       └─────────┘
                         ♠ J 5 2
                         ♡ J 10 6 3
                         ◊ A J 5
                         ♣ 7 6 5
```

S We need four tricks

T We tally our sure tricks:

Spades:	2 winners: the ♠A and ♠K
Hearts:	1 winner: the ♡A
Diamonds:	0 winners
Clubs:	0 winners

O We organize our plan.

Since we have only three tricks, we'll need to use our imagination to see where we can find one more. It doesn't look as if we can get any more tricks from spades, hearts or clubs, so it will have to be the diamond suit. It should be possible if my partner has either the ◊A or ◊K, as long as we don't wait too long. Otherwise, the declarer may be able to discard his diamond losers.

P We put the plan into operation.

We win the first trick with the ♠K and lead a diamond. There is no need to take the ♠A right away. My partner will realize that we have the ♠A when our ♠K wins the first trick. On the actual hand, my partner wins with the ◊K and then leads another spade. Our ♡A defeats the contract.

If we had taken both our spade tricks before making a plan, the declarer could make the contract. When we then led a diamond, the declarer could win the ◊A and discard the dummy's remaining diamond on his established ♠J. Oops!

CHAPTER 3

Sure Tricks

Bridge is luck, skill and your relationship with your partner. Never underestimate the importance of the power of this connection with the person sitting opposite you.

The defenders may sometimes have enough sure tricks to defeat the contract, but taking them may not be so easy.

Taking your sure tricks

Consider the following suit that you and your partner hold when defending against a no-trump contract:

	N	
You	W E	Partner
♡ Q 8 3	S	♡ A K J 10 2

If you were the declarer, you would have no trouble seeing that you have five sure tricks in this suit. You would also have no difficulty in taking the tricks. You could start by playing the *high card* from the *short side*, the queen and then playing a small card to your partner's remaining high cards.

As a defender, the situation is much more complex. First, you cannot see your partner's hand. Looking at only your cards, it is impossible to know that your side has five tricks in the suit. You might choose to lead a completely different suit. Even if you choose to lead the suit, you may not get all the tricks you are entitled to. Suppose you lead a small card and your partner wins the first two tricks with the ace and king and then leads a small card back to your queen. Now you are on lead and your partner's remaining winners are *stranded* unless he has an *entry* (a winner in another suit).

If you are defending against a suit contract, there are additional difficulties. Even if you could see your partner's cards, you would not know how many sure tricks you had without some additional information. After all, the declarer could have a singleton, or even a void. You may have no sure tricks in the suit.

The situation is far from hopeless, however. You can get clues from the auction – both from the bids made by your side and those made by your opponents. This will help you plan the defence and decide which cards to play during the hand. Next, there are a number of guidelines to help you when you have no other information to go on. Finally, you and your partner can help each other through the use of *signals*. You can give information through the specific card you choose to play in a suit.

In this chapter, we'll look at some examples of how the defenders co-operate to make sure they get the tricks to which they are entitled. In later chapters, we'll develop these concepts in more detail. The most important thing to remember is that you have to use your imagination. To compensate for the declarer's advantage of being able to see both his hand and the dummy, you will have to try to visualize the layout of the missing cards. With a little practice, you'll soon find yourself defending as though you could see right through the backs of the cards.

Leading your partner's suit

Where are you going to start looking for your side's sure tricks when they are not staring you in the face? If your partner has bid a suit during the auction, perhaps when opening the bidding or making an overcall, a good place to start looking is your partner's suit. In fact, unless you have a clearly better alternative, a good guideline is: **lead your partner's suit**.

To make sure that you get the sure tricks you are entitled to, you have to be careful in choosing the card you lead. Suppose this is the layout:

```
                    N
        You     ┌───────┐  Partner
        ♡ A 4   │ W   E │  ♡ K Q J 10 2
                │   S   │
                └───────┘
```

If you lead the ♡4, your partner can win the first trick and lead another heart which you win with the ♡A. You have taken the first two tricks but you are now on lead. Your partner cannot take the rest of his sure tricks in the suit. Instead, you want to use the same principle that the declarer uses in this situation. You start by leading the ♡A, the high card from the short side. Now you can play the ♡4 over to your partner and he can take the rest of his sure tricks in the suit. For a full explanation of this principle, read Zia's book *Collins Bridge for Beginners: Declarer Play*.

Notice that you cannot actually see your partner's cards when you lead the ♡A. Instead, you are visualizing the potential layout of the missing cards that will allow you to take your side's sure tricks in the suit. As a general rule, always lead the **top of a doubleton in your partner's suit**. Let's see how this works out when you have to make an opening lead from the following hand:

♠ 8 7 3
♡ J 7
◊ 10 9 8 7 2
♣ 9 6 5

The opponents have reached a contract of 3NT after your partner opened the bidding with 1♡. You should lead your partner's suit. With a doubleton, you follow the guideline of leading the top card, the ♡J. Here is the complete hand:

Contract: 3NT

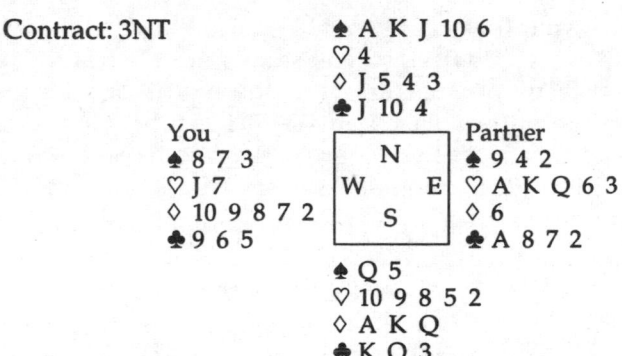

```
                    ♠ A K J 10 6
                    ♡ 4
                    ◊ J 5 4 3
                    ♣ J 10 4
    You                               Partner
    ♠ 8 7 3          ┌─────────┐      ♠ 9 4 2
    ♡ J 7            │    N    │      ♡ A K Q 6 3
    ◊ 10 9 8 7 2     │ W     E │      ◊ 6
    ♣ 9 6 5          │    S    │      ♣ A 8 7 2
                     └─────────┘
                    ♠ Q 5
                    ♡ 10 9 8 5 2
                    ◊ A K Q
                    ♣ K Q 3
```

Your ♡J wins the first trick and, when you lead another heart, your partner takes the ♡A, ♡K, ♡Q, ♡6 and ♣A to defeat the contract by two tricks. If you had led a diamond, the declarer would make the contract, taking five spade tricks and four diamond tricks. If you had led the ♡7 instead of the ♡J, your partner would have won the first trick – but look what happens now! If he returns a small heart, you can win with the ♡J but have no more hearts to lead to your partner's hand. And if your partner instead leads the ♡A or ♡K to the second trick, your ♡J will crash underneath it and establish a winner for declarer's ♡10. Remember – in order to follow the principle of playing the high card from the *short side* in our side's long suits, we must lead the top card from a doubleton in partner's bid suit.

Leading your own suit

Suppose you end up defending against a no-trump contract and your partner has not bid a suit. Now, you might have to look for sure tricks from one of your own suits. It is not difficult to see where the sure tricks are coming from if you have a suit headed by the ace, king and queen, for example, but what if your suit looks like this:

♠ A Q 8 4 2

This is where you are going to have to use your imagination. If you need to get a lot of tricks from this suit, you will have to visualize that your partner holds the ♠K. If that is the case, how should you go about taking your tricks in the suit? You want to play the high card from the short side first, so you should start by leading a small spade. When your partner wins the first trick with his (hoped for) ♠K, he will be able to lead a small spade back to you so that you can take the rest of your sure tricks. You hope the complete layout of the suit is something like this:

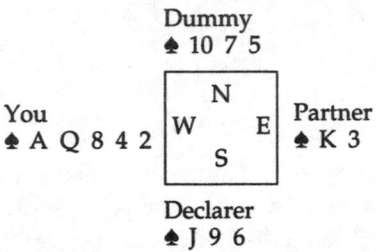

Dummy
♠ 10 7 5

You
♠ A Q 8 4 2

Partner
♠ K 3

Declarer
♠ J 9 6

Note that if you started by leading the ♠A and then a spade to your partner's ♠K, your partner would have no spade left to lead back to your ♠Q. Of course your partner may not have the ♠K but, as we shall see later, it may still be a good idea to start off by leading a low spade when you are going to need some help from your partner in the suit.

Sometimes, you cannot afford to lead a low card, even when you are missing one or more high cards. Suppose you have this suit:

♢ K Q J 10 2

If you were sure that your partner held the ♢A, you could lead a small diamond and your partner could lead a diamond back so that you would get five sure tricks in the suit. Unfortunately, you cannot see your partner's cards and it is unlikely that you can be certain that your partner holds the ♢A. If the declarer holds the ♢A and you lead a small diamond, the declarer may win the trick with the ♢9 and still have the ♢A. As we shall see in the next chapter, in situations where you have a strong sequence of cards, it is usually best to lead one of your high cards. In the above example, if the declarer does hold the ♢A, you will at least prevent him from winning a trick with a smaller diamond and holding on to his ♢A for later.

When you lead from a strong sequence of cards, you lead the top of your *touching cards*, the ◇K in the above example. Why? Remember our earlier comment about giving information to your partner. By always leading the top card of a sequence, you tell your partner that you do not have the next higher card, but you do have the next lower card. In the above example, leading the ◇K tells your partner that you do not have the ◇A, the next higher card, but you do have the ◇Q, the next lower card. All of a sudden your partner has information about the location of three cards.

Leading the top of a sequence can help the partnership take its sure tricks in this type of situation:

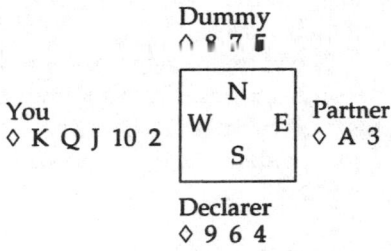

Dummy
♠ 9 7 5

You
◇ K Q J 10 2

N
W   E
S

Partner
◇ A 3

Declarer
◇ 9 6 4

You can see that you have five sure tricks in the diamond suit but actually taking them at the table might not be so easy. If you start by leading the ◇K and your partner lets you win the first trick, you can lead a second diamond to his ◇A. Once again, however, you have ended in the wrong hand at the wrong time.

How can this be prevented? By leading the ◇K, you are telling your partner that you have the ◇Q and possibly the ◇J as well, since you are leading the top of a strong sequence, rather than leading a low card. Now it is your partner's turn to use his imagination. He can visualize your holding in the suit and he knows that the defence wants to start by winning with the high card from the short side. Instead of letting you win the first trick with the ◇K, he can *overtake* it with his ◇A and then lead back the ◇3 to the rest of your sure tricks. The technical term for this type of play is *unblocking the suit* since the suit would be blocked if your partner had only the ◇A left with no small card to lead to your winners.

The declarer would have had an easy time taking five tricks with the above combination of cards. But the defenders can accomplish the same task with the use of a little imagination and ingenuity.

Summary

The defenders take their sure tricks in the same way that the declarer does. Whenever possible, they want to start by leading the high card(s) from the short side so that they can then lead a small card over to the remaining winners on the long side. Unfortunately, since they cannot see each other's cards, it is more difficult for the defenders to determine whether or not they have sure tricks in a suit and, even then, they may have to be careful to ensure that they get all their tricks.

The defenders have to use their imagination to help visualize where sure tricks are coming from. They get their clues from the auction, from the cards their partner leads and from the cards their partner plays during the hand. In the end, you will often find that two heads are better than one!

Over Zia's shoulder

Hand 1 Dealer: North

North	East	South	West
			(Zia)
1◇	1♡	1♠	Pass
2♣	Pass	2NT	Pass
3NT	Pass	Pass	Pass

```
            (Zia)
            ♠ J 10 9 6 2    ┌─────────┐
            ♡ K 6           │    N    │
            ◇ 7 6           │ W     E │
            ♣ J 10 9 7      │    S    │
                            └─────────┘
```

Here I am on lead against 3NT and my best suit appears to be spades. I also have a nice-looking sequence in clubs. Should I start by leading a spade, or are there other things I should be thinking about? I'd better STOP and make my plan before I do the wrong thing.

Solution to Hand 1:

Contract: 3NT

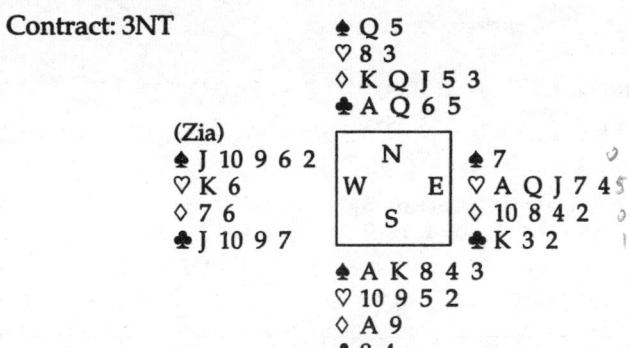

```
                    ♠ Q 5
                    ♡ 8 3
                    ◊ K Q J 5 3
                    ♣ A Q 6 5
      (Zia)
   ♠ J 10 9 6 2    N        ♠ 7
   ♡ K 6        W     E     ♡ A Q J 7 4 5
   ◊ 7 6           S        ◊ 10 8 4 2
   ♣ J 10 9 7               ♣ K 3 2
                    ♠ A K 8 4 3
                    ♡ 10 9 5 2
                    ◊ A 9
                    ♣ 8 4
```

S Stop to consider the goal. We are going to need five tricks to defeat 3NT.

T Tally the winners. We don't have any sure tricks in our hand.

O Organize the plan. With no winners in our hand, we are going to have to find some. I'm going to need help from my partner, so which suit offers the most promise? Although spades is our best suit, we must remember to listen to the auction. My partner overcalled in hearts, so that is where his length and strength is likely to be. With no clearly better alternative, I should lead my partner's suit, hearts.

P Put the plan into operation. With a doubleton in my partner's suit, I lead the top card, the ♡K. On the actual hand, this works very nicely. My partner lets us win this trick and I continue with the ♡6 over to my partner's remaining winners. We get the first five tricks and defeat the contract.

If I had not led a heart, the declarer would make the contract, taking three spade tricks, five diamond tricks and a club trick. It is always important to listen to what your partner has said during the auction. Also, if I had led a small heart, my partner could win the trick and lead a heart back to my ♡K, but we would be in the wrong hand to take the rest of our winners. By leading the ♡K, we tackle the suit by playing the high card from the short side first.

Hand 2 Dealer: East

North	East (Zia)	South	West
	Pass	1♡	Pass
3♡	Pass	4♡	Pass
Pass	Pass		

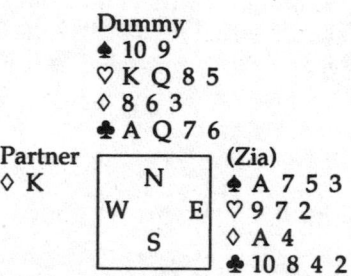

Dummy
♠ 10 9
♡ K Q 8 5
◇ 8 6 3
♣ A Q 7 6

Partner
◇ K

(Zia)
♠ A 7 5 3
♡ 9 7 2
◇ A 4
♣ 10 8 4 2

It looks as though my partner has made a good lead. If the declarer has no singletons or voids, we should have two sure tricks in diamonds and one in spades. But where is the *setting trick* (by 'setting trick' I mean the trick that will defeat, or *set*, the contract) going to come from?

Solution to Hand 2:

Contract: 4♡

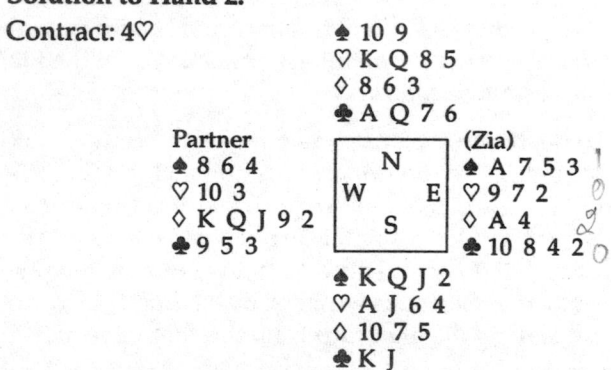

♠ 10 9
♡ K Q 8 5
◇ 8 6 3
♣ A Q 7 6

Partner
♠ 8 6 4
♡ 10 3
◇ K Q J 9 2
♣ 9 5 3

(Zia)
♠ A 7 5 3
♡ 9 7 2
◇ A 4
♣ 10 8 4 2

♠ K Q J 2
♡ A J 6 4
◇ 10 7 5
♣ K J

S We need four tricks to defeat 4♡.

T Tally the sure tricks:
 Spades: 1 winner (the ♠A)
 Hearts: 0 winners
 Diamonds: 2 winners: (the ◊A and my partner's ◊K)
 Clubs: 0 winners

O Organize the plan. Since we have only three tricks, we must use our imagination to see where we can find one more. My partner's lead of the ◊K has given a clue. Since he leads the top of touching high cards when he has a sequence, he should have the ◊Q and, perhaps, the ◊J as well. If the declarer has three diamonds in his hand, we are entitled to three sure tricks in the suit to go along with our ♠A.

P Put the plan into operation. We have to be careful to ensure that we get all our diamond tricks. On my partner's ◊K, I will have to play the ◊A, so that I will have a small diamond left to lead back to my partner's winners. Otherwise, the suit will be blocked. On the actual hand, this lets us take the first three diamond tricks and then a spade trick.

If I let my partner's ◊K win the first trick, the declarer makes the contract. My partner can lead a diamond to my ◊A, but we have no way to get our other diamond trick. The declarer will eventually discard his remaining diamond on one of the dummy's club winners.

CHAPTER 4

Promoting High Cards

Staring at either your partner or the opponents should be avoided.

As we saw in the previous chapter, the defenders sometimes have enough sure tricks to defeat the contract. All they have to do is be careful to take them. More often, however, they will need to develop some of the winners they will need in order to defeat the contract. When a declarer needs extra tricks, one of his most straightforward options is to develop them through *promotion*. There is nothing to stop the defenders from using the same technique.

Promoting winners

When you have a series, or *sequence*, of touching high cards, you have a good opportunity to promote winners. Consider this suit:

♠ K Q J 10 9

If the declarer has the ♠A, you do not have a single sure trick. There is, however, a lot of potential to develop winners. You can lead the ♠K – remember, you lead the top of your touching high cards to help tell your partner what you have – and drive out the ♠A. You will end up promoting your remaining cards in the suit into four winners.

You will not always be dealt such a powerful sequence. Nevertheless, promoting winners when you have a sequence is an excellent source of tricks. Look at this holding:

♡ Q J 10 9 8

Even if the other side has both the ♡A and ♡K, your side has the potential to enjoy three tricks from this suit. You would have to give the lead up twice but, with a little patience, you will eventually develop some winners. Notice that you will have to give up the lead to the declarer when you are trying to promote tricks. You have no choice, however, if that is the only way you can get enough winners to defeat the contract. Don't be afraid to give up the lead, if it will help you reach your objective.

There may be times when you have to give up the lead as many as three times in order to promote the winners you need. For example, suppose you are on lead against a contract of 3NT with the following hand:

♠ J 10 9 8 7
♡ A 6 3
◊ A 5
♣ A 8 5

You need five tricks to defeat the contract but you only have three sure tricks. Where can the extra winners come from? It may seem like a lot of work, but you should be able to promote the winners you need in the spade suit. Let's look at the complete hand and see what happens if you start off by leading the top of your sequence, the ♠J:

Contract: 3NT

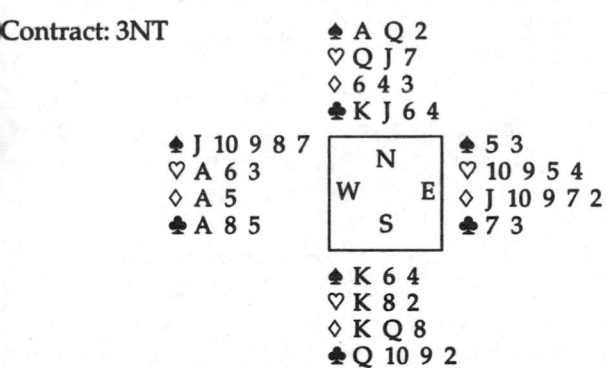

```
                    ♠ A Q 2
                    ♡ Q J 7
                    ◊ 6 4 3
                    ♣ K J 6 4
   ♠ J 10 9 8 7    ┌─────────┐   ♠ 5 3
   ♡ A 6 3         │    N    │   ♡ 10 9 5 4
   ◊ A 5           │ W     E │   ◊ J 10 9 7 2
   ♣ A 8 5         │    S    │   ♣ 7 3
                   └─────────┘
                    ♠ K 6 4
                    ♡ K 8 2
                    ◊ K Q 8
                    ♣ Q 10 9 2
```

The declarer has the top three cards in the spade suit but, if you are persistent, you can prevail. The declarer can win the first trick but he also needs to promote some winners to make the contract. Suppose he leads a club. You win with the ♣A and lead another spade, driving out his second winner in the suit. When the declarer leads a heart, to develop winners in that suit, you win and lead a spade once more. This drives out the declarer's remaining high card in the suit. He still does not have enough winners to make the contract. When he finally leads a diamond, you win with the ◊A and take your two promoted spade winners to set the contract.

Many hands are similar to this. It is a race between the declarer and the defenders to see which side can develop the tricks they need first. The defenders will not always win the race. They do, however, have the advantage of the opening lead. They can strike the first blow.

Preserving entries

In the above hand, it was important that you led spades every time you had the lead and that you held on to your aces in the other suits. Each ace was an *entry* to your hand, a winner that let you get the lead. Entries are important to the defenders, especially when they are trying to promote winners. To promote winners, you have to give up the lead to the declarer. You will need entries, therefore, to regain the lead and let you take your winners once they are established.

On the above hand, look what would happen if you had started by taking your three aces before you led spades. You would get the first three tricks but the declarer would now be able to take the rest. By taking your aces, you would be promoting winners for the declarer, rather than helping the defence.

How do you know when to take your winners and when to hold on to them as entries? After all, in the previous chapter we saw that the defenders must sometimes take their sure tricks in order to defeat the contract. The secret is always to make your plan. Your plan will tell you how many winners you need to defeat the contract. If you have enough winners, go ahead and take them. If you do not, your priority is to develop the extra winners you need, not to take your sure tricks.

Getting help from your partner

When promoting tricks, you do not need all the high cards in the same hand. Consider this layout when defending against a no-trump contract:

```
            N
You       ┌─────┐   Partner
♣K J 9 5 2 │W   E│  ♣Q 10 6
           └─────┘
              S
```

The only high card missing is the ♣A, so you should be able to develop four sure tricks through promotion. The difficulty, of course, is that you cannot see your partner's hand. How do you know that he has the ♣Q and ♣10? You cannot be sure. This is where you have to rely on your imagination once again. You have to visualize the high clubs in your partner's hand. Once you have done that, how do you actually go about promoting the tricks? Remembering the principle of playing the high card from the short side first, you want to use your partner's high card(s) first, so that he will have a small card left to lead back to your winners. You do this by leading a low card initially. This is the same way that a declarer would tackle the suit.

Although you cannot see your partner's cards, leading a low card from a suit in which you do not have a strong sequence will work well against a no-trump contract in a number of situations. For example, the complete layout of the suit might actually be something like this:

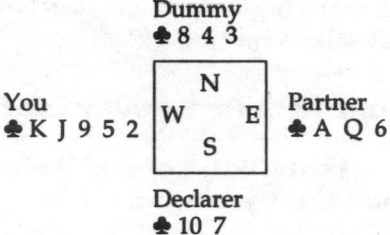

Dummy
♣ 8 4 3

You
♣ K J 9 5 2

Partner
♣ A Q 6

Declarer
♣ 10 7

In this case, you are not actually promoting tricks. Instead, you are taking your sure tricks. You could not tell, when you led your low card, which would be the case. In fact, your partner might have neither the ♣A nor the ♣Q. Even so, as we shall see in later chapters, leading a low club may work out well.

In promoting winners in a suit when the high cards are divided between the two hands, the partners must co-operate. If one partner starts leading a suit, trying to promote winners, and the other partner gains the lead, he should return his partner's suit unless he has a clearly better alternative. Otherwise, the partnership will be working at cross-purposes. The partnership does not usually have the time or resources for each partner to promote his own suit. The partner making the opening lead has set the direction and, unless it becomes clear that things have got off on the wrong foot, both partners should work together on the same plan for defeating the contract. Here is an example in a complete hand:

Contract: 3NT

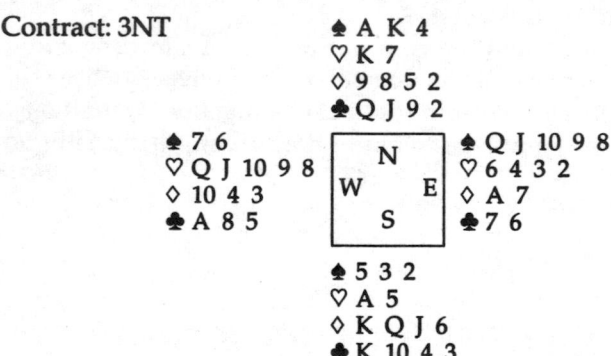

♠ A K 4
♡ K 7
◇ 9 8 5 2
♣ Q J 9 2

♠ 7 6
♡ Q J 10 9 8
◇ 10 4 3
♣ A 8 5

♠ Q J 10 9 8
♡ 6 4 3 2
◇ A 7
♣ 7 6

♠ 5 3 2
♡ A 5
◇ K Q J 6
♣ K 10 4 3

West gets off to the opening lead of the ♡Q, top of a sequence, planning to promote winners in the suit. The declarer wins the first trick with the ♡A and leads the ◊K, trying to promote his own winners in order to make the contract. What does East do when he wins the ◊A? East has his own spade suit in which he would like to promote winners, but it is too late for that. If East leads a spade, the declarer wins the trick and drives out West's ♣A. Whether West leads a heart or a spade, the declarer can win and take enough tricks to make the contract.

Instead, East must work with West to finish promoting the heart suit. After winning the ◊A, East leads another heart, driving out the dummy's ♡A. When the declarer leads a club, West can now win the ♣A and take his three promoted heart tricks to defeat the contract.

Putting it into practice

Having seen some of the ways you can go about developing tricks through promotion, let's see how you would choose the card to lead against a contract of 3NT with each of the following hands. We will assume that you have chosen to lead a spade. In later chapters, we will look further at the reasons you might choose a spade rather than one of the other suits.

1	♠ QJ1096	2	♠ Q10863	3	♠ QJ863
	♡ K72		♡ K72		♡ K72
	◊ 84		◊ 84		◊ 84
	♣ A95		♣ A95		♣ A95

In the first hand, lead the ♠Q, top of the touching cards in your strong sequence. Even if your partner has neither the ♠A nor ♠K, you should eventually be able to promote some winners in the suit. You do not want to lead your ♠6 in case the declarer can win the first trick with the ♠8 and still have the ♠A and ♠K left.

In the second hand, you do not have a strong sequence. You are going to need some help from your partner to promote tricks in the suit. Start by leading a low spade. With luck, your partner will have the ♠A, ♠K or ♠J and will be able to help you out. He may even hold two of these cards, making your task easier.

In the last hand, you have two touching cards but it is not really a strong sequence. It looks as though you are going to need some help from your partner to promote winners in the suit. Lead a low card. You are hoping that your partner holds the ♠A, ♠K or ♠10 to help you promote winners in the suit.

Summary

Promotion is one of the techniques the defenders can use to develop the tricks they need to defeat a contract. With a strong sequence of high cards, you generally lead the top of your touching cards. This helps to give your partner the information he needs to co-operate in promoting the tricks. Without a strong sequence, you will need help from your partner. In this case, you can lead a low card. The idea is to ensure that you get the (hoped for) high card(s) from the short side played first.

You will usually have to help when your partner is trying to promote winners. An important guideline to keep in mind is to return your partner's suit, unless you clearly have something better to do. This avoids the problem of working at cross-purposes with your partner's plan.

Over Zia's shoulder

Hand 1 Dealer: East

North	East	South	West
			(Zia)
	Pass	1♠	Double
2♠	Pass	3♠	Pass
4♠	Pass	Pass	Pass

```
                (Zia)
                ♠ A K          ┌─────────┐
                ♡ 8 6 4 2      │    N    │
                ◊ Q J 1 0      │ W     E │
                ♣ A 7 6 3      │    S    │
                               └─────────┘
```

Despite my *takeout double*, the opponents have bid on to game. How can I teach them to have a little more respect when I come into the auction? (For an explanation of the takeout double read Zia's book *Collins Bridge for Beginners: Bidding*.)

Solution to Hand 1:

Contract 4♠

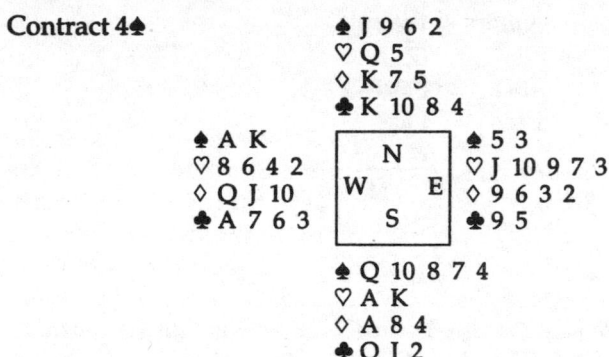

```
                    ♠ J 9 6 2
                    ♡ Q 5
                    ◇ K 7 5
                    ♣ K 10 8 4
      ♠ A K                          ♠ 5 3
      ♡ 8 6 4 2         N            ♡ J 10 9 7 3
      ◇ Q J 10      W       E        ◇ 9 6 3 2
      ♣ A 7 6 3         S            ♣ 9 5
                    ♠ Q 10 8 7 4
                    ♡ A K
                    ◇ A 8 4
                    ♣ Q J 2
```

S Stop to consider the goal. We need four tricks to defeat the 4♠ contract.

T Tally the winners. We have two sure tricks in spades and one in clubs.

O Organize the plan. We are going to have to find one more winner. Looking at the diamond suit, there is the possibility for promoting a trick in the suit, even if the declarer has both the ◇A and ◇K. This looks like our best choice. Developing a trick in another suit would require my partner to hold some strength, unlikely when the opponents have bid a game and we hold as much as we do.

P Put the plan into operation. When promoting tricks, it is best to get started as soon as possible, keeping our other high cards as entries. I start by leading the ◇Q, top of my sequence. The declarer can win the first trick and start to draw trumps. I'll win a spade trick and play another diamond, promoting my remaining diamond into a winner. When we regain the lead, we can take our diamond trick to defeat the contract.

If we had not gone about promoting a diamond trick, the declarer would make the contract. He would eventually discard one of his diamond losers on the dummy's extra club winners once our ♣A had been driven out.

Hand 2 Dealer: South

North	East	South	West
			(Zia)
		1NT	Pass
3NT	Pass	Pass	Pass

(Zia)
♠ K J 9 6 2
♡ 10 8 2
◇ 9 5
♣ A 8 3

Here I am defending another game. I've only got one sure trick to take. I'd better STOP and make a plan to decide how best to go about defeating this contract.

Solution to Hand 2:

Contract: 3NT

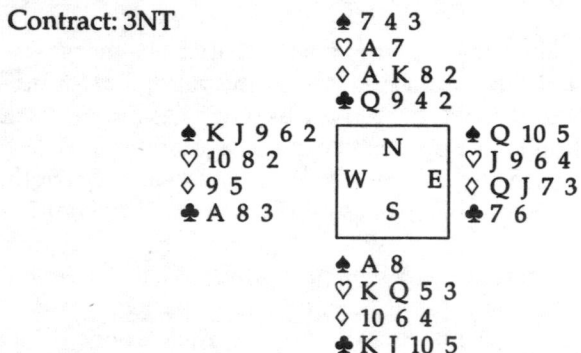

♠ 7 4 3
♡ A 7
◇ A K 8 2
♣ Q 9 4 2

♠ K J 9 6 2
♡ 10 8 2
◇ 9 5
♣ A 8 3

♠ Q 10 5
♡ J 9 6 4
◇ Q J 7 3
♣ 7 6

♠ A 8
♡ K Q 5 3
◇ 10 6 4
♣ K J 10 5

S Stop to consider the goal. We will need five sure tricks to defeat the 3NT contract.

T Tally the winners. We have only one sure trick, the ♣A.

O Organize the plan. I do not have a suit in which I can promote the winners we need all by myself. It looks as though I will need some help from my partner. Putting our imagination to work, we should be able to promote some tricks in the spade suit if my partner has one or more of the missing high spades. That suit offers the best possibility since any other suit will require a lot more help from my partner.

P Putting the plan into action, I lead a low spade. If my partner does have the help I need, I want to start by playing the high card from the short side, which should be my partner's side when we have length in the suit. On the actual hand, this works like a charm. My partner has the ♠Q, enough to help us drive out the declarer's ♠A. When we regain the lead with the ♣A, we can take our four promoted tricks in the spade suit.

If I was afraid to lead a spade on this hand, in case my partner did not have any help in the suit, we would never have defeated the contract. The declarer would drive out our ♣A and have an easy time taking nine tricks.

CHAPTER 5

Establishing Small Cards

Remember at the bridge table you want to meet old friends and make new ones ... not lose friends.

There are five *honours* in each suit – the ace, king, queen, jack and ten – and eight small cards – the nine down to the two. It is not often that the defenders have enough combined strength to defeat the contract with their high cards alone. It is important to remember, however, that a small card can have the same power as an honour if it can be established as a winner. This is especially valuable in a no-trump contract, since the declarer will have no trump suit to prevent you from taking a winner once it is established. Let's consider how you can defend by making the best use of the small cards.

Establishing tricks in long suits

Consider the layout of the following suit:

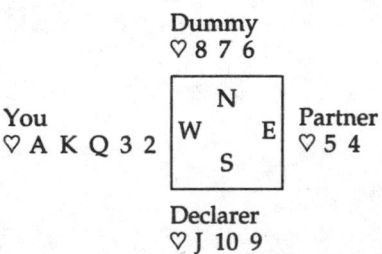

You initially have only three sure tricks, the ♡A, the ♡K and the ♡Q. After you have played the suit three times, however, none of the other players has any hearts left. If the contract is in no trumps, you can now take two more tricks, the ♡3 and the lowly ♡2. The small cards in your long suit have become established as winners.

As we have seen in previous chapters, the high cards do not all have to be in the same hand for the defenders to have the opportunity to establish their small cards. Look at this layout:

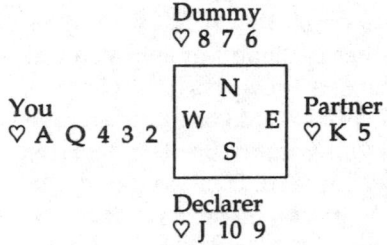

The situation is virtually identical. This time, however, you will have to start by leading a small card to your partner's ♡K and he can then return his small card back to your winners. We have seen in earlier chapters that leading a small heart from your holding is not unusual. It is the same thing you have to do when taking sure tricks or promoting winners, in order to get the high card played from the short side first.

Giving up the lead

You do not necessarily need any high cards in a suit in order to develop tricks through length. Look at this example:

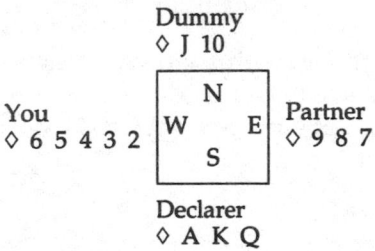

Although the declarer has all the honours in the suit, you can still develop two winners in the suit by leading it three times. Each time you lead the suit, one of the declarer's high cards disappears until, finally, no one has any diamonds left and your remaining two diamonds are winners.

To develop winners in this manner takes some patience and some luck. You must keep leading the suit at every opportunity. You must also be fortunate enough to have high cards in other suits with which to regain the lead each time you give it up. You don't always have to do all the work by yourself. If your partner has high cards in other suits he can help you out by leading diamonds every time he gets the opportunity to lead.

The moral, however, is not to be afraid to give up the lead if it will get you where you want to be. The declarer will frequently have to give you back the lead. Don't forget that the declarer is also trying to develop the tricks he needs and this will occasionally involve losing the lead to the defenders.

Considering the division of the missing cards

How many tricks can you expect to get from your small cards? That depends on how the missing cards are *divided* among the remaining hands. Suppose we return to an earlier example:

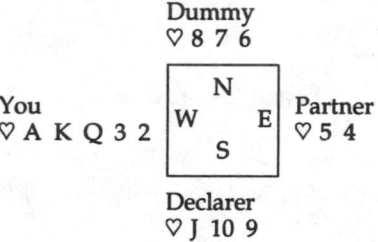

Dummy
♡ 8 7 6

You
♡ A K Q 3 2

Partner
♡ 5 4

Declarer
♡ J 10 9

In this layout, you end up with five tricks – two from small cards – because the opponents' hearts are divided 3-3 (three in one hand, three in the other). Suppose we change the layout slightly:

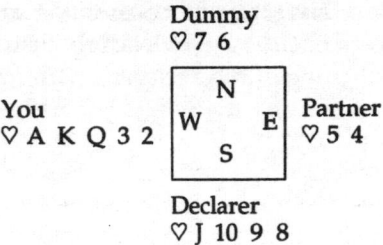

With the opponents' hearts divided 4-2, you can only take the first three sure tricks before the declarer will have a winner left in the suit. You can still establish one trick through length by leading the suit again to drive out the declarer's winner. Now, let's change the distribution a bit more:

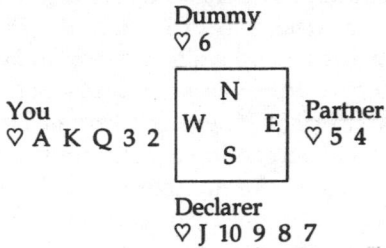

If this is the layout of the heart suit, you never get more than your three sure tricks. You cannot get any tricks with your small cards.

In general, what can you expect? Will the missing cards be divided as they are in the first case, the second, or the third? You would like to have some idea of what to expect so that you will know whether or not there is a reasonable chance of developing the tricks you need from a particular suit.

If you know how many cards the opponents hold in a suit, you can determine their most likely division using the following chart:

Expected Division of Opponents' Cards

Number of cards held	Most likely distribution
3	2-1
4	3-1
5	3-2
6	4-2
7	4-3
8	5-3

You don't need to memorize the chart. It is enough to notice the general concept: an even number of cards tend to divide unevenly, an uneven number of cards tend to divide evenly.

It is much more straightforward for a declarer to make use of such a chart than for a defender. After all, a declarer can see both his hand and the dummy. A defender will usually be uncertain how many cards his partner has in a suit and will, therefore, be uncertain how many cards are held by the opponents.

On the other hand, a defender sometimes has an advantage over a declarer in this respect. If he can determine how many cards his partner has, he can determine exactly how many cards the declarer has by looking at the number of cards in the dummy. Sometimes, you can get a clue from the auction to how many cards your partner has in a suit. Later, when you look at the chapter on signals, you will see how the defenders can sometimes tell each other exactly how many cards they have in a suit.

Knowing about the likely division of the missing cards can help you decide which suit to lead when you have a choice. Suppose the auction proceeds as follows:

North	East	South	West
			(You)
		1NT	Pass
3NT	Pass	Pass	Pass

After this uninformative auction, you find yourself on lead with the following hand:

♠ A 8 6 3
♡ A 7 5 4 2
◇ 7 2
♣ 8 5

With only two sure tricks, you are going to have to find three extra tricks from somewhere. It looks as though both the spade suit and the heart suit have some potential for developing extra tricks through length, but which suit should you lead? Here is where you can put your imagination to work. You cannot see your partner's hand so you are going to have to visualize what he might hold. Let's make a reasonable assumption that he holds three or four small cards in both suits. Now, which suit presents the better potential?

If your partner has three spades, the opponents have six spades between them. The most likely division is for an even number of missing cards to divide unevenly, 4-2, so one of the opponents is likely to have four spades. This makes it unlikely that you can get an extra trick through length. Even if your partner has four spades, there is only potential for one extra trick through length.

Turning our attention to the heart suit, the potential for extra tricks through length is much better. Now, even if your partner has only three small cards, there is a good chance for two extra tricks in the suit. The complete layout of the suit might look something like this:

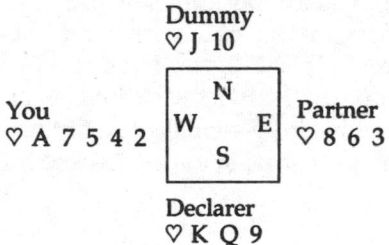

Dummy
♡ J 10

You
♡ A 7 5 4 2

N
W   E
S

Partner
♡ 8 6 3

Declarer
♡ K Q 9

You have one sure trick and, by leading the suit twice more, can develop two extra tricks from length.

The conclusion is that the longer the suit, the more potential for developing tricks through length. Given two suits of equal strength, you should lead your longer suit if you are planning to develop tricks from length. This applies most often when you are defending against a no-trump contract. Against a suit contract, developing extra winners in a long suit is often not very useful, since the declarer will be able to trump them.

Getting to your winners

In order to enjoy the winners you have developed in a suit, you have to regain the lead so that you can take them. You need an entry to your winners. One reason why established small cards sometimes do not end up taking tricks is that they become stranded – the defender who has the entry is not the defender who holds the winners. How can the defenders avoid this problem?

Once again, the answer lies in using a lot of imagination. Let's suppose you are on lead with the following hand against a contract of 3NT:

♠ A 8 7 6 3
♡ 7 4
♢ 9 6 2
♣ 8 7 5

In making your plan, you know that your side has to take five tricks in order to defeat the contract. You have only one sure trick, the ♠A. Somehow, your side has to take four more tricks. Where can they come from? You are not sure how the missing spades are divided but, if you assume that your partner has three and that the opponents' cards are divided 3-2, you could end up with two winners from your small cards after the suit has been played three times. That's fine, but in order to make use of these winners you have to be able to get to them. Let's suppose that this is the layout of the spade suit:

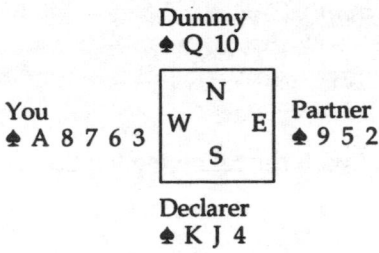

Dummy
♠ Q 10

You
♠ A 8 7 6 3

Partner
♠ 9 5 2

Declarer
♠ K J 4

To establish your small cards as winners, the suit will have to be played three times. Suppose you start off by leading the ♠A and another spade. The declarer will win the second trick and go about his business. If he has to give up a trick to East, your partner can lead another spade to drive out the declarer's last spade and establish your two remaining spades as winners. But they are stranded. You have no entry with which to regain the lead. Even if your partner manages to regain the lead, he has no spades left to lead to your winners.

To get round this problem you must start by leading a *low* spade, giving the first trick up to the opponents. If your partner wins a trick and leads another spade, you still must not take your ♠A. Instead, you must *duck* – let the opponents win a trick which you could have won. Now the situation is completely different. If your partner regains the lead, he still has a spade left to lead to your ♠A. Your small cards are established and you can take your winners.

You have preserved your ♠A as an entry to your winners. Essentially, you have merely changed the order in which you gave up the spade tricks. Instead of playing the ♠A and then giving up two spade tricks, you have given up two spade tricks and then taken the ♠A. This little change in order makes all the difference. As a defender, you should keep the following principle in mind: if you have to lose one or more tricks to the declarer when establishing long cards in a suit, it is usually best to lose the tricks as early as possible.

Let's see how this principle can be applied when the auction has proceeded:

North	East	South	West
			(You)
		2NT	Pass
3NT	Pass	Pass	Pass

and you have to lead with the following hand:

♠ A K 9 8 4
♡ J 4 2
◇ 9 4
♣ 9 7 5

With only two sure tricks, the best hope for developing additional tricks appears to be in the spade suit. Your partner could hold the ♠Q, or may hold some length. In either case, you can give your side the best chance to defeat the contract by leading a small spade. If your partner has the ♠Q, so much the better. If not, you are losing the trick you have to lose as early as possible. Here is the complete hand:

Contract: 3NT

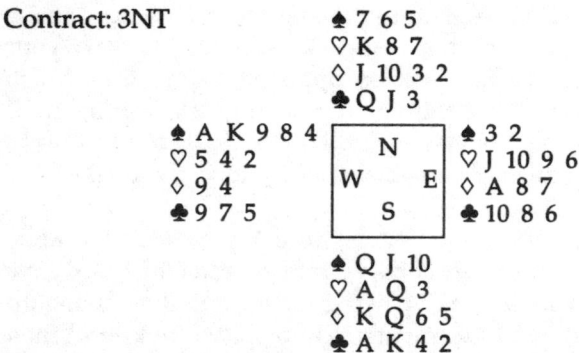

                    ♠ 7 6 5
                    ♡ K 8 7
                    ◇ J 10 3 2
                    ♣ Q J 3

♠ A K 9 8 4   ♠ 3 2
♡ 5 4 2   N   ♡ J 10 9 6
◇ 9 4   W   E   ◇ A 8 7
♣ 9 7 5   S   ♣ 10 8 6

                    ♠ Q J 10
                    ♡ A Q 3
                    ◇ K Q 6 5
                    ♣ A K 4 2

Your partner has a rather disappointing holding in the spade suit and, when you lead a small spade, the declarer can win the first trick with the ♠10. All is not over, however. The declarer, needing to establish winners in the diamond suit, leads a diamond and your partner takes the trick with the ◇A. He has a spade left to lead back and you can take the ♠A and ♠K. No one else has any spades left and you can now take your remaining two small spades to defeat the contract.

What if you had started off by leading the ♠A and ♠K? You could still establish your remaining small spades as winners by leading the suit again, but it would not do you any good. When the declarer leads a diamond and your partner takes his ◊A, your partner has no spade left to lead back to you. You have no entry left to your hand. Whatever suit your partner leads, the declarer can win and take the rest of the tricks, making the contract.

Summary

When you are looking for ways to develop the additional winners needed to defeat a contract, consider the possibility of developing winners from the small cards in your long suits. The longer your suit, the more potential for developing winners.

When developing cards in long suits, always consider the division of the missing cards in the opponents' hands. In general, an odd number of missing cards will tend to divide as evenly as possible and an even number of missing cards will tend to divide unevenly. For example, five missing cards will tend to be divided 3-2, rather than 4-1 or 5-0; six missing cards will tend to be divided 4-2, rather than 3-3, 5-1 or 6-0.

You will usually have to give up tricks to the declarer in order to establish your small cards in a suit. Consider how you are going to get to your winners once they are established. You will need an entry. If you have to give up tricks to the declarer, it is usually best to lose the tricks as early as possible, holding on to your high cards as entries.

Over Zia's shoulder

Hand 1 Dealer: South

North	East	South	West
			(Zia)
		1NT	Pass
3NT	Pass	Pass	Pass

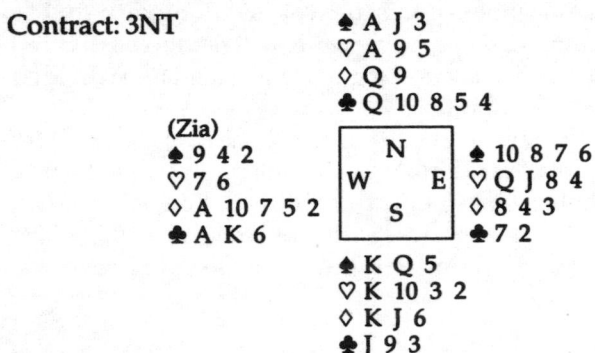

(Zia)
♠ 9 4 2
♡ 7 6
◇ A 10 7 5 2
♣ A K 6

I can see three sure tricks against the opponents' 3NT contract. Where are tricks four and five going to come from?

Solution to Hand 1:

Contract: 3NT

♠ A J 3
♡ A 9 5
◇ Q 9
♣ Q 10 8 5 4

(Zia)
♠ 9 4 2   ♠ 10 8 7 6
♡ 7 6   ♡ Q J 8 4
◇ A 10 7 5 2 ◇ 8 4 3
♣ A K 6   ♣ 7 2

♠ K Q 5
♡ K 10 3 2
◇ K J 6
♣ J 9 3

S Stop to consider the goal. We need five tricks to defeat the 3NT contract.

T Tally the winners. We have one sure trick in diamonds and two in clubs.

O Organize the plan. We are going to have to find two more winners. Although our high cards in clubs are attractive, our long diamond suit offers the better potential to develop tricks from length, without too much help from our partner. I think we should start by leading a small diamond.

P Put the plan into operation. On the actual layout, the declarer wins the first diamond trick and, needing to develop some club tricks make the contract, leads a club. We win the club trick and lead diamonds again. Holding the ♣A as an entry, we can afford to lead the ◊A and another diamond to establish our remaining small diamonds as winners. The declarer is helpless. When he leads another club, we win and take our diamonds to defeat the contract.

Notice how important it was to keep our ♣A and ♣K as entries. If we had taken them early, we would be doing the declarer's work for him – establishing winners in the club suit. Instead, we go about our business of setting up some extra diamond winners.

Hand 2 Dealer: East

North	East	South	West
			(Zia)
	Pass	1NT	Pass
3NT	Pass	Pass	Pass

Dummy
♠ K 5
♡ 9 8 6
◊ K Q J 10 5
♣ Q J 10

(Zia)
♠ 10 9 8
♡ J 7 5 3
◊ 2
♣ A 9 8 5 4

```
        N
    W       E
        S
```

After making my plan, I decide to lead a small club, hoping to develop some extra tricks in my club suit from the small cards. Of course, I'll need a little help from my partner ... but that is what partners are for! After I lead a club, the dummy comes down and my partner wins the first trick with the ♣K and, being a good partner, returns my suit by leading another club. Well, now I can see two sure tricks for the defence but it looks as though the dummy is going to get a club trick. Where are the rest of our tricks going to come from?

Solution to Hand 2:

Contract: 3NT

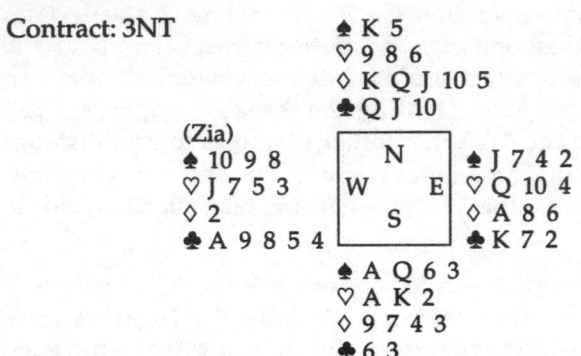

```
                    ♠ K 5
                    ♡ 9 8 6
                    ◇ K Q J 10 5
                    ♣ Q J 10
    (Zia)
    ♠ 10 9 8            N          ♠ J 7 4 2
    ♡ J 7 5 3     W          E     ♡ Q 10 4
    ◇ 2                S          ◇ A 8 6
    ♣ A 9 8 5 4                    ♣ K 7 2
                    ♠ A Q 6 3
                    ♡ A K 2
                    ◇ 9 7 4 3
                    ♣ 6 3
```

S Stop to consider the goal. We need five sure tricks to defeat the 3NT contract.

T Tally the winners. We have only one sure trick, the ♣A.

O Organize the plan. Looking at my hand, the best chance to develop extra tricks appears to be in the club suit. Since I have five clubs, I may be able to develop some tricks through length if my partner has three or four clubs.

P Put the plan into operation. Putting our plan into action, I lead a small club and my partner wins the first trick with the ♣K and returns a club. Things have got off to a good start but this is where we must be careful. If we win this trick and lead another club, we will drive out the dummy's last club and establish our remaining two clubs as winners. But how will we regain the lead to take our winners? We have no entry. Instead of winning the second trick, we must play a small card, letting the dummy win the trick and keeping our ♣A as an entry. On the actual hand, the declarer wins the second club trick and has to lead a diamond to establish the winners he needs. Fortunately, our partner can win this trick with the ◇A and has a small club left to lead to our ♣A and we can now take our two established winners to defeat the contract.

We needed a little luck to defeat the contract – my partner held the ◇A and three clubs. But, without our careful play, we would have had no chance at all.

CHAPTER 6

The Finesse in Defence

At the bridge table, the president of a company and the mail clerk are equal.

A *finesse* is an attempt to take a trick with a card when the opponents hold a higher card. For example, you may want to try to win a trick with the king when the opponents hold the ace, or win a trick with the queen when the opponents hold the ace or king or both, or even win a trick with the jack when the opponents have the ace, king or queen. Instead of focusing on how the number of missing cards are divided, as you did when looking for tricks through length, you have to focus on the location of the missing high cards when trying to get extra tricks from finesses. Let's start by considering a simple finesse: when the missing high card is in the dummy and both you and your partner can see it.

Finessing against a high card in the dummy

Once the dummy has been put down on the table, the defenders can see the location of some of the high cards that their side is missing. In some respects, this can make it easier for the defenders than for the declarer when it comes to taking a finesse. Consider this situation, where your partner has led the ♠3 against the declarer's contract:

Dummy
♠ K 9

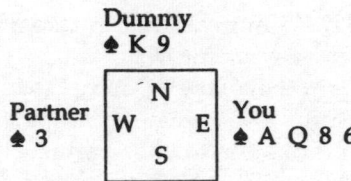

Partner   You
♠ 3   ♠ A Q 8 6

If the declarer plays the ♠9 from the dummy, you can see that you only need to play the ♠Q to win the trick. The dummy's ♠K is *trapped* by your ♠A and ♠Q. There are many similar types of situations that will arise in defence. For example, let's change the cards in the dummy and your hand slightly:

Dummy
♠ Q 9

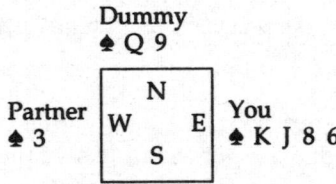

Partner   You
♠ 3   ♠ K J 8 6

You do not really care where the ♠A is. Suppose the declarer has it. If the declarer plays the dummy's ♠Q, you will play your ♠K and, if the declarer wins the trick with the ♠A, your ♠J has become a winner. If the declarer plays the ♠9 from the dummy, you will finesse the ♠J, forcing him to win the trick with the ♠A and making your ♠K a winner.

Repeating a finesse

Just as a declarer can repeat a finesse, so can the defenders. Take a look at this layout where your partner has led the ♡2:

Dummy
♡ K 9 7

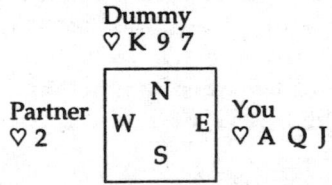

Partner   You
♡ 2   ♡ A Q J

If the declarer plays the dummy's ♡K, you can win the ♡A and take tricks with your ♡Q and ♡J. But suppose the declarer plays a small heart from the dummy. You can take a finesse, which you know will work, by playing the ♡J.

Although you could play the ♡Q rather than the ♡J, you should generally win the trick by playing only as high a card as necessary in order to give information to your partner. When your ♡J wins the trick your partner will know that you hold the ♡Q as well since otherwise the declarer would have won the trick with that card. On the other hand, if you win the first trick with the ♡Q, your partner will probably think that the declarer holds the missing ♡J.

Once you win the first trick, what do you do next? If you play the ♡A, you will establish the declarer's ♡K as a winner. Unless you are sure that only two heart tricks will be enough to defeat the contract, you will probably want to get three heart tricks from this layout. That means that you want to repeat the finesse. You can only repeat the finesse by switching to another suit and waiting until your partner (or the declarer) leads hearts again. You can see the advantage of winning the first trick with the ♡J. When your partner regains the lead, he will know that you still have the ♡A and ♡Q left and he can lead another heart.

Let's put this idea into action on a complete hand after the auction has gone:

North	East	South	West
(Dummy)	(You)	(Declarer)	(Partner)
1◊	1♡	1♠	Pass
3♠	Pass	4♠	Pass
Pass	Pass		

Your partner leads the ♡4, the suit you bid, and the dummy comes down:

Contract: 4♠

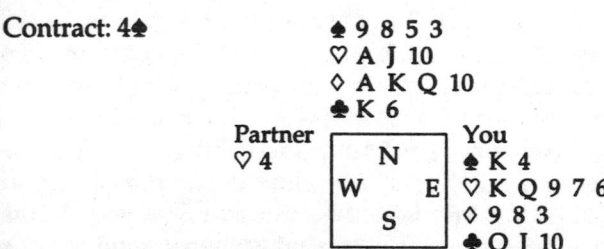

```
                    ♠ 9 8 5 3
                    ♡ A J 10
                    ◊ A K Q 10
                    ♣ K 6
        Partner  ┌─────────┐  You
        ♡ 4      │    N    │  ♠ K 4
                 │ W     E │  ♡ K Q 9 7 6
                 │    S    │  ◊ 9 8 3
                 └─────────┘  ♣ Q J 10
```

The declarer plays the ♡10 from the dummy on the first trick and what do you do? It's time to STOP and make your plan. You need four tricks to defeat the contract and it looks as though you are going to win the first heart trick. Where are the other tricks going to come from? You might be able to get a second heart trick, but you cannot lead another heart from your side of the table since the ♡A and ♡J are still left in the dummy. It looks as though you are going to need your partner to have a high card in spades or clubs to help you out. To put your plan into action, you must win the first trick with the ♡Q so that your partner will know that you also have the ♡K and, when he regains the lead, he can co-operate with your plan for defeating the contract.

After winning the first trick with the ♡Q, you lead back a club, hoping that your partner has the ♣A and can win and lead another heart through the dummy. A club is probably a better choice than a spade since, if your partner has a trick in the trump suit, he will get it anyway, as soon as the declarer starts *drawing trumps*. Let's look at the complete hand:

Contract: 4♠

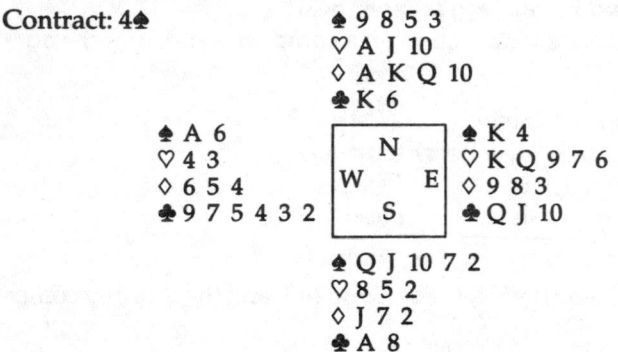

```
              ♠ 9 8 5 3
              ♡ A J 10
              ◇ A K Q 10
              ♣ K 6
♠ A 6                        ♠ K 4
♡ 4 3           N            ♡ K Q 9 7 6
◇ 6 5 4      W     E         ◇ 9 8 3
♣ 9 7 5 4 3 2     S          ♣ Q J 10
              ♠ Q J 10 7 2
              ♡ 8 5 2
              ◇ J 7 2
              ♣ A 8
```

It turns out that your partner does not have the ♣A but has the ♠A instead. That is still good enough to defeat the contract. The declarer wins the club trick and starts drawing trumps by leading a spade. Your partner wins the ♠A and, visualizing the situation in the heart suit, leads his remaining small heart through the dummy. The declarer is helpless. If he plays the dummy's ♡J, you will win the ♡K and, if he plays the dummy's ♡A, your ♡K is established as a winner which you can take when you win a trick with the ♠K. It does the declarer no good to win the dummy's ♡A and start playing diamonds before giving you a trick with the ♠K, hoping to discard his heart loser on the dummy's fourth diamond. Your partner will be able to trump the last diamond with the ♠6 and the contract will still be defeated.

Leading a high card through the dummy

The defender's high cards do not all need to be in one hand in order to trap a missing high card. Consider this situation:

```
              Dummy
              ◇ K 8 3
                  N
  Partner       W   E    You
  ◇ Q J 10 9       S     ◇ A 4 2
              Declarer
              ◇ 7 6 5
```

Your partner can lead the ◇Q, top of a sequence, and the dummy's ◇K is trapped. If the declarer plays the dummy's ◇K, you can win the trick with the ◇A and the defenders have the rest of the tricks in the suit. If the declarer plays a small card from the dummy, you can play one of your small cards, letting your partner's ◇Q win the trick.

The importance to the defenders of always leading the top of touching high cards can be illustrated by making the situation a little more complicated. Let's look at this layout of the cards where your partner leads the ◇J:

```
              Dummy
              ◇ K 8 3
                  N
  Partner       W   E    You
  ◇ J 10 9 7       S     ◇ A 4 2
              Declarer
              ◇ Q 6 5
```

There is no problem for the defenders if the declarer plays the ◊K from the dummy. You can win the ◊A and lead the suit back, restricting the declarer to one diamond trick, the ◊Q. What if the declarer plays a small diamond from the dummy, rather than the ◊K? You know from your partner's lead of the ◊J that the declarer holds the ◊Q, since your partner always leads the top of his touching cards. Does that mean you should take the ◊A to prevent the declarer from winning the first trick with the ◊Q?

Look at what happens if you do play the ◊A on the first trick. The declarer will play a small diamond from his hand and will end up with two tricks in the suit, the ◊K and the ◊Q. Instead, suppose you do not play the ◊A on the first trick. The declarer wins with the ◊Q but now has only one trick in the suit since the remaining cards look like this:

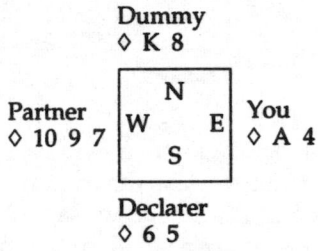

The dummy's ◊K is now trapped. When your partner regains the lead, he can lead the ◊10 or ◊9 and the declarer cannot get any more diamond tricks. If he plays the ◊K, you win the ◊A and if he plays a low diamond, you let your partner's high diamond win the trick. Here is a similar example in a complete hand where the auction has gone:

North	East	South	West
(Dummy)	(You)	(Declarer)	(Partner)
		1♡	Pass
4♡	Pass	Pass	Pass

Your partner leads the ♠J and this is the complete layout:

Contract: 4♡

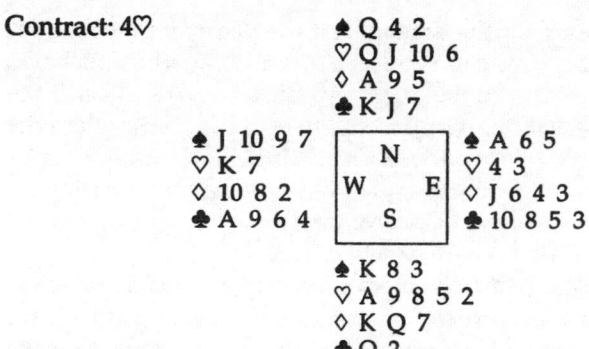

When the declarer plays a small spade from the dummy on the first trick, you must be careful not to play the ♠A. The declarer will win the first trick with the ♠K, but now you have the dummy's ♠Q trapped. When the declarer leads a club, your partner can take the ♣A and lead another high spade. Whether the declarer plays the dummy's ♠Q or a small card, the defenders get two spade tricks. Eventually, your partner also gets a trick with the ♡K and the contract is defeated. If you play the ♠A on the first trick, the declarer ends up making the contract, losing only one spade trick, one heart trick and one club trick.

Trapping the declarer's high cards

The defenders, of course, can trap high cards in the declarer's hand as well as those in dummy. The difficulty in this situation, however, is that they cannot actually see the high card(s) in the declarer's hand and, instead, must try to visualize them. Sometimes it is easy. Consider the following layout of the club suit when defending against a no-trump contract:

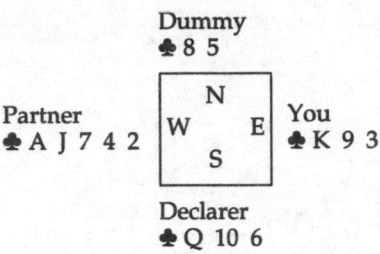

Dummy
♣ 8 5

Partner
♣ A J 7 4 2

You
♣ K 9 3

Declarer
♣ Q 10 6

We have seen in earlier chapters that it is a good idea when defending against a no-trump contract to lead a low card from a long suit, rather than a high card, when you do not have a strong sequence. This is to allow the high card to be won from the short side first when taking sure tricks and to preserve an entry to your long suit when trying to establish winners through length. It also works well in this type of situation, when the defenders need to take a finesse.

Your partner leads a small club and you win the first trick with the ♣K. When you lead a club back, the declarer's ♣Q is trapped. Whether he plays the ♣Q or ♣10, your partner gets the rest of the tricks in the suit. If your partner had started by leading the ♣A, he could continue by leading a small club to your ♣K, but now you could no longer trap the declarer's ♣Q.

In the above situation, you did not consciously have to think about trapping a high card in the declarer's hand. After all, you were merely returning your partner's suit. Your partner might have held both the ♣A and ♣Q, in which case you would be helping to take your side's sure tricks. Your partner might have held the ♣Q, and the declarer the ♣A, in which case you would be helping to promote tricks in your partner's hand by driving out the declarer's ♣A. Or your partner might have held neither the ♣A nor ♣Q, in which case you would be helping your partner develop tricks from his length in the suit.

Nevertheless, there are times when you must visualize how you might be able to trap the unseen high cards in the declarer's hand. Since you can only see the high cards in the dummy, you usually follow the guideline of *leading through strength and up to weakness* in such situations. That is, you try to lead through the declarer's (assumed) strength and up to the weak holding in the dummy. For example, your partner leads the ♡J after the following auction:

North	*East*	*South*	*West*
(Dummy)	(You)	(Declarer)	(Partner)
1◇	Pass	1♠	Pass
3♠	Pass	4♠	Pass
Pass	Pass		

Contract: 4♠

```
                        ♠ A J 6 5
                        ♡ K Q
                        ◇ K Q 10 8
                        ♣ J 7 6
        Partner       ┌─────────┐   You
          ♡ J         │    N    │   ♠ 10
                      │ W     E │   ♡ A 6 5 4
                      │    S    │   ◇ 7 5 4 3
                      └─────────┘   ♣ 10 9 8 2
```

The declarer plays the ♡Q from the dummy and you must STOP to figure out what your plan is. You need four tricks and have only one sure trick yourself, so it looks as though your partner is going to have to provide the others. Where can they come from? Whatever tricks your partner may have in the trump suit he is sure to get eventually. There is not much future in the heart suit, since the dummy has the ♡K and will be able to trump hearts, even if you drive out that card. It looks as though the tricks will have to come from diamonds or clubs. Which suit should you lead? Here is where you have to try to visualize the high cards in the declarer's hand. If he has a high card in diamonds, there is not much you can do, but if he has a high card in clubs, you might be able to trap it by leading through his (supposed) strength and up to the club weakness in the dummy.

Following your plan, you win the ♡A and lead back a club. This is the complete hand:

Contract: 4♠

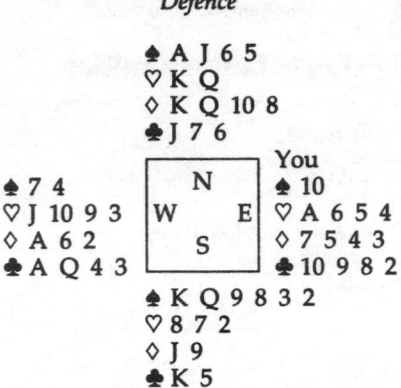

When you return a club, the declarer's ♣K is trapped. Whether the declarer plays the ♣K or ♣5, your partner gets two tricks in the suit. He also takes the ◊A, to defeat the contract. What if you had not led back a club but had led another heart instead? The declarer would win the trick, draw trumps and lead a diamond to drive out your partner's ◊A. Your partner could no longer trap the declarer's ♣K. If he took the ♣A, the declarer's ♣K would be promoted. If he did not take the ♣A, the declarer would be able to discard his club losers on the dummy's extra diamond winners. To defeat the hand, you had to lead through the declarer's strength.

Summary

A finesse is an attempt to win a trick with a high card when the opponents hold a higher card in the suit. In order to do this, you usually need to lead towards the card you hope will take the trick. With a strong sequence, you can sometimes lead the top of your touching cards to help your partner trap the opponents' high cards. Both defenders need to keep their eyes open for opportunities to trap the opponents' high cards.

It is easier to trap a high card which you can see in the dummy rather than an unseen high card in the declarer's hand. The defenders can use the principle of *leading through strength and up to weakness* to help guide them when it is difficult to visualize the exact layout of the missing cards.

Over Zia's shoulder

Hand 1 Dealer: East

North	East (Zia)	South	West
	Pass	Pass	Pass
1NT	Pass	2♡	Pass
Pass	Pass		

Dummy
♠ A Q J 6
♡ 10 9 7
◇ A K 8
♣ 9 5 4

Partner
♠ 2

(Zia)
♠ K 9 3
♡ K 6
◇ 10 7 5 2
♣ Q J 10 8

Finally, my opponents have stopped in a partscore contract. That doesn't mean I plan to relax. Every hand is important. It hurts my pride – and, sometimes my wallet – whenever I fail to defeat a contract that can be beaten. The declarer plays the ♠J on the first trick. What's my plan going to be?

Solution to Hand 1:

Contract: 2♡

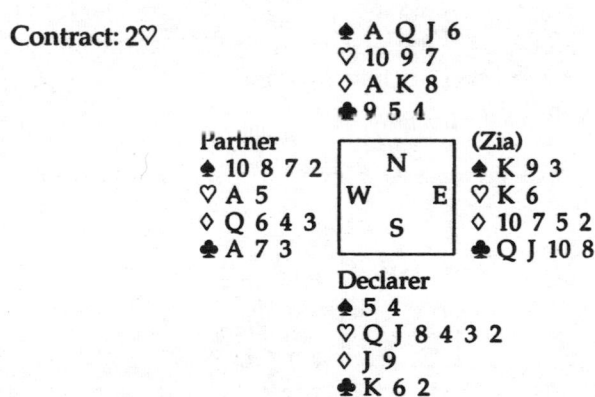

♠ A Q J 6
♡ 10 9 7
◇ A K 8
♣ 9 5 4

Partner
♠ 10 8 7 2
♡ A 5
◇ Q 6 4 3
♣ A 7 3

(Zia)
♠ K 9 3
♡ K 6
◇ 10 7 5 2
♣ Q J 10 8

Declarer
♠ 5 4
♡ Q J 8 4 3 2
◇ J 9
♣ K 6 2

S We need six tricks to defeat 2♡.

T When the declarer plays the dummy's ♠J on the first trick, we can see one sure trick in spades.

O I am going to need some help from my partner if we are to develop enough tricks to defeat the contract. He might have a trump trick or two, but he will get them no matter what I do. I am going to have to find some tricks from the club suit. I cannot see the high cards in the declarer's hand but I can use the idea of leading through strength to try to trap a high card in his hand.

P Having decided where our tricks might come from, we win the first trick with the ♠K and lead back the ♣Q, top of our sequence, hoping to trap the ♣K in the declarer's hand. On the actual layout of the cards, this works well. We are able to take three club tricks and eventually get the ♡A and ♡K as well, enough to defeat the contract.

If I had not visualized the possibility of trapping a high card in the declarer's hand, we would not have defeated the contract. If we lead back a spade or a diamond, the declarer can win the trick and discard one of his small clubs on the dummy's extra spade winner. Now it is too late for the defence to get all three of its club tricks.

Hand 2 Dealer: West

North	East (Zia)	South	West
			Pass
1♣	Pass	1♡	Pass
4♡	Pass	Pass	Pass

Dummy
♠ Q 8 4
♡ A Q 6 5
◊ 9
♣ A K Q 10 2

Partner
◊ J

	N		(Zia)
W		E	♠ K J 5 3
	S		♡ 10 3
			◊ A 7 5 2
			♣ 9 5 4

The opponents are back to normal, bidding all the way to a game contract. That's a pretty nice-looking dummy. Do we have a chance?

Solution to Hand 2:

Contract: 4♡

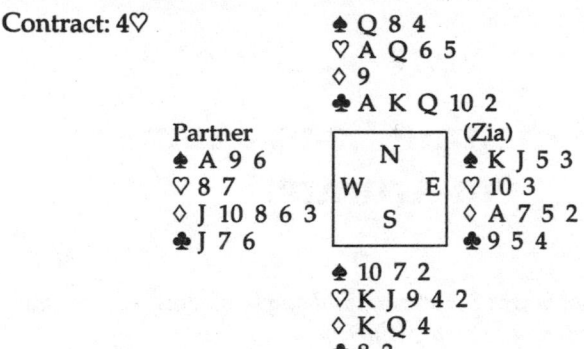

```
                    ♠ Q 8 4
                    ♡ A Q 6 5
                    ◇ 9
                    ♣ A K Q 10 2
Partner                              (Zia)
♠ A 9 6          ┌─────────┐        ♠ K J 5 3
♡ 8 7            │    N    │        ♡ 10 3
◇ J 10 8 6 3     │ W     E │        ◇ A 7 5 2
♣ J 7 6          │    S    │        ♣ 9 5 4
                 └─────────┘
                    ♠ 10 7 2
                    ♡ K J 9 4 2
                    ◇ K Q 4
                    ♣ 8 3
```

S We are going to have to find four tricks to defeat 4♡.

T The only sure trick we have is the ◇A.

O Since my partner has led the top of his touching high cards, I know that the declarer will be able to win the first trick with the ◇Q unless we take the first trick with the ◇A. After that, the declarer will be able to trump any losing diamonds in the dummy. It doesn't look as though we are going to get any tricks from hearts or clubs, so our best hope must be in the spade suit. Perhaps my partner holds the ♠A. In that case, I should be able to trap the dummy's ♠Q if my partner helps me out.

P Putting the plan into operation, I win the first trick with the ◇A and lead back a small spade to my partner's (hoped for) ace. When my partner wins the ♠A on the actual hand, he too will have to visualize the finesse situation and lead back a spade so that I can take two more spade tricks by trapping the dummy's ♠Q.

This is the only defence to beat the contract. If I had led back anything else but a small spade, the declarer would have had no trouble taking the rest of the tricks.

CHAPTER 7

The Opening Lead against No-Trumps

Bridge is a sport that you can start as a child and be playing with as much enthusiasm and skill when you are ninety.

Now that we have seen some of the ways in which the defenders can get tricks, it is time to turn our attention to the specific task of selecting an opening lead. The opening lead must be chosen before the dummy is seen, reducing the amount of information the defender has available. Once the opening lead has been made and dummy has gone down, the defenders are in a better position to make a complete plan for defeating the contract.

For this reason, we sometimes modify our STOP mnemonic to think in these terms when we are making an opening lead:

S – stop to review the bidding
T – think about the best lead
O – organize your plan
P – put your plan into operation

In this chapter, we'll use this approach to see how we go about selecting the best lead against a no-trump contract. In a later chapter, we'll look at the differences when we have to make the opening lead against a suit contract.

Reviewing the bidding

Before choosing your opening lead, you should always STOP and review the bidding. It is amazing how much information about the other players' hands you can get from the auction, even before you see the dummy. Taking the time to try to visualize the hands will help you throughout the defence. As you see more and more cards, you can update your mental picture until it is as though you are seeing through the backs of the hidden cards.

For example, if one of the other players has bid a suit during the auction, he will usually have at least four cards in the suit. If your partner has overcalled in a suit, you can expect him to have at least five cards in the suit. If an opponent has bid and rebid a suit, without support from his partner, he will have at least a five-card suit and probably more. If his partner fails to support the suit, especially in the case of a major suit, it is probably because he has only one or two cards in the suit. If a player describes a balanced hand, perhaps by opening or rebidding in no trumps, you can be certain that he has no singletons or voids, and probably only one doubleton.

Similarly, when someone opens the bidding at the one level, he probably has a hand of 12 or more points. If he subsequently makes a minimum raise of his partner's response or rebids his suit at the lowest available level, he probably has a hand of about 12–15 points. If he makes a jump raise of the responder's suit or jumps to the three level in his own suit, he probably has a medium-strength hand of about 16–18 points. If the opener jumps in a new suit or takes the responder right to game after a one-level response, he probably has a maximum hand of about 19–21 points.

You can also draw information from what the opponents do not do during the auction. If they stop in a partscore contract, they likely have fewer than 26 combined points. If they stop in a game contract, they probably have fewer than the combined 33 points required for a small slam. If an opponent passes originally and then bids strongly thereafter, he probably has 10–11 points, not quite enough to open the bidding.

Let's look at some examples of the type of picture you can draw. Suppose you are West and the auction proceeds as follows:

North	East	South	West
			(You)
1◊	Pass	1♡	Pass
2◊	Pass	2NT	Pass
3NT	Pass	Pass	Pass

What do we know about North's hand? He must have four diamonds and 12 or more points to open the bidding 1◊ and, since he bid them again without support, he must have at least five of them. He did not support his partner's heart suit at any point in the auction so he must have three or fewer hearts. He did not bid 1♠ or 2♣ at his second opportunity, so he is unlikely to have four cards in either of these suits. He also did not open 1NT or rebid 1NT, so he does not have a balanced hand. What about his strength? He made a minimum rebid at his first opportunity, so we can expect about 12–15 points. He did, however, accept his partner's invitational bid of 2NT by raising to game. So North should be at the top of his range, 14 or 15 points, counting points for his long suit. We might expect the dummy to come down looking something like this:

♠ A 4 3
♡ Q 5
◊ A K 10 9 4 2
♣ 9 7

What about the declarer's (South's) hand? He will have at least four hearts for his 1♡ response, but is very unlikely to have as many as six of them, since he did not try to suggest that suit as trumps once his partner failed to show support at the first opportunity. His no-trump rebid suggests a balanced hand. With an unbalanced hand, he might have bid another suit or supported the opener's diamond suit. As far as his strength is concerned, he did not pass the opener's minimum rebid but also did not go all the way to game, choosing an invitational rebid of 2NT instead. This implies that he has about 11–12 points, enough to invite the opener to carry on to game. A hand consistent with South's bidding would be something like this:

♠ K J 5
♡ K 9 8 3
◊ 7 5
♣ A 8 6 4

We even know something about our partner's hand! He does not have a good enough suit or enough points to enter the auction with an overcall or takeout double after the 1◊ bid. Negative inferences such as this can sometimes be as important as the positive ones gained from the bids made.

Thinking about the best lead

Let's review the earlier auction when the opponents reached 3NT:

North	East	South	West
			(You)
1◊	Pass	1♡	Pass
2◊	Pass	2NT	Pass
3NT	Pass	Pass	Pass

Forming a mental picture of the missing hands helps you decide what to lead when you have a hand such as the following:

♠ 10 6 2
♡ A J 2
◊ Q 8 3
♣ Q 10 5 2

The picture you have constructed from the bidding steers you away from considering a heart or diamond lead, since those are the suits bid by the opponents. It comes down to a choice between the black suits. You need less help from your partner in the club suit than the spade suit, especially since he did not have enough to make an overcall in spades. You reach the conclusion that a club would be the best lead. You are rewarded when the complete hand turns out to be:

Contract: 3NT

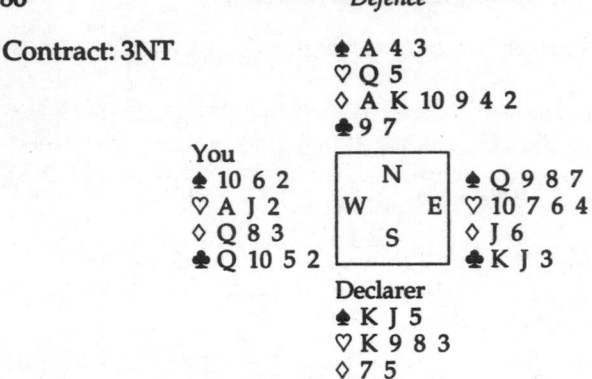

♠ A 4 3
♡ Q 5
◊ A K 10 9 4 2
♣ 9 7

You
♠ 10 6 2
♡ A J 2
◊ Q 8 3
♣ Q 10 5 2

♠ Q 9 8 7
♡ 10 7 6 4
◊ J 6
♣ K J 3

Declarer
♠ K J 5
♡ K 9 8 3
◊ 7 5
♣ A 8 6 4

On a club lead, the defenders are able to promote three club tricks by driving out the declarer's ♣A. The declarer has to give up a diamond trick in order to develop the tricks he needs and the defence ends up with a heart trick, a diamond trick and three club tricks. Did you see through the backs of the cards? Not quite, but you defended as though you had. If you had led any other suit, the declarer would have had no trouble making the contract.

When choosing the suit to lead against a no-trump contract, you usually want to try to find the longest combined suit in the partnership hands. The longer the suit, the more potential for establishing the tricks you need to defeat the contract.

To help find the best suit to lead, consider the following guidelines:

- **Lead your partner's suit** – if your partner has opened the bidding or overcalled, unless you clearly have a better alternative. The reason for this is that your partner will have some length in the suit he bid and is likely to have more high cards than you. His high cards will serve as entries to help develop tricks in his long suit.
- **Avoid leading a suit bid by the opponents.** It is unlikely that you are going to find much help in your partner's hand if the opponents have bid a suit you are considering leading. Unless you have a very strong sequence to lead from, you are more likely to help the declarer by leading one of his suits. After all, the declarer may also need to get tricks from that suit to make

his contract. It cannot be right for both sides to want to attack the same suit.
- **Lead your longest suit if there is nothing else to go on.** Your longest suit has the best chance of being the longest combined suit in the partnership hands and, therefore, of having the best potential for developing the number of tricks you need.
- **Lead the stronger suit if there is a choice of equally long suits** – since you will need less help from your partner to develop winners in the suit.

Let's look at a practical example by considering the following hand from which you have to make a lead against the opponents' 3NT contract:

♠ 96
♡ K 10 8 5 2
♢ 6
♣ J 10 6 3 2

If your partner has opened the bidding 1♠, or overcalled in spades during the auction, you should lead your spade since you do not have a clearly better alternative. You are hoping to develop tricks in your partner's suit and that he will have an entry so that he can take them once they are established.

If the opponents had bid hearts during the auction, you should avoid leading that suit and, instead, pick the longer of your remaining suits, clubs. If the opponents did not bid anything during the auction, you would choose the stronger of your two five-card suits and lead hearts.

As you can see from this example, you cannot choose the suit to lead until you have first reviewed the auction.

Choosing the card to lead

Once you have selected the suit you are going to lead, you must choose the specific card in the suit that you are going to lead. From the discussions in previous chapters, we can draw up the following guidelines for leading against no-trump contracts:

When leading partner's suit:
- Lead the top of a doubleton (9 2, Q 3)
- Lead the top of touching high cards (Q J 10, J 10 9)
- Otherwise, lead low (Q 7 2, K 8 4 3)

When leading your own suit:
- Lead the top of a three-card or longer sequence
  (K Q J 7, Q J 10 8 2)
- Lead the top of an *interior sequence* (K J 10 9, A 10 9 8 5)
- Lead the top of a *broken sequence* (K Q 10 8, Q J 9 6 2)
- Otherwise, lead low (fourth best) (K J 8 5, A 10 8 4 3)

Let's review the reason for each of these leads in turn. You lead the top of a doubleton in your partner's suit to avoid blocking the suit. You want to make sure that the high card gets played from the short side first. For example:

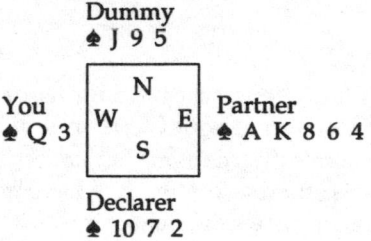

Dummy
♠ J 9 5

You
♠ Q 3

Partner
♠ A K 8 6 4

Declarer
♠ 10 7 2

By leading the ♠Q, the defence can take the first five tricks. The situation would be similar if you were promoting tricks, rather than taking sure tricks:

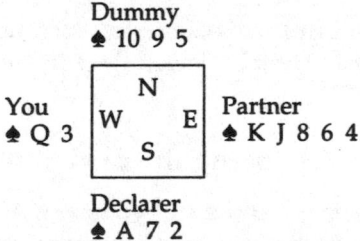

Dummy
♠ 10 9 5

You
♠ Q 3

Partner
♠ K J 8 6 4

Declarer
♠ A 7 2

If you were to lead a low spade first and your partner's ♠K drove out the declarer's ♠A, your partner could lead a small spade back to your ♠Q when he regained the lead. But your partner's remaining winners would be stranded unless he has an entry in another suit.

You lead low from three or more cards for two reasons. It helps your partner distinguish between the case where you hold a doubleton and where you hold three or more cards, since you would lead the top card from a doubleton, rather than a low card. It may also help the defenders trap cards in the declarer's hand. For example:

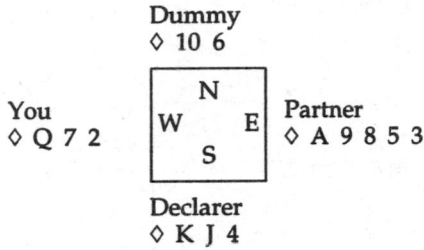

When you lead the ◊2, your partner can win the first trick with the ◊A and lead a diamond back, trapping the declarer's ◊J. On the other hand, if you had led the ◊Q, the declarer would end up with two tricks in the suit.

When leading your own suit, you lead the top of a three-card or longer sequence to prevent the declarer from winning a cheap trick in the suit. For example:

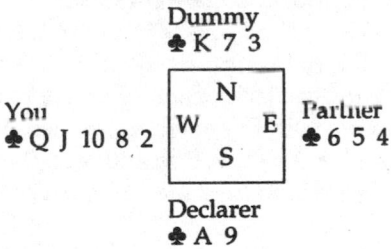

If you were to lead a low club, the ♣2 or ♣8, the declarer would win the first trick with the ♣9 and still have the ♣A and ♣K left for two more tricks. By leading the ♣Q, you force the declarer to win the trick with one of his high cards. You can subsequently lead the

♣J or ♣10 to drive out the declarer's other high card and establish the remainder of your clubs as winners.

Another reason for leading the top of your touching cards is to give your partner information. He knows you have the next lower card but not the next higher card. You tell him about the location of three cards all at the same time.

An interior sequence is one in which you have two or more touching cards and you also have a higher card in the suit. Leading the top of your touching cards helps trap cards in either the declarer or the dummy's hand. For example:

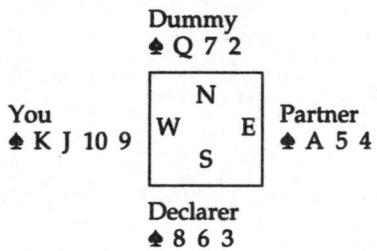

Dummy
♠ Q 7 2

You
♠ K J 10 9

Partner
♠ A 5 4

Declarer
♠ 8 6 3

When you lead the ♠J, the dummy's ♠Q is trapped. If the declarer plays the ♠Q, your partner wins the ♠A and you get four tricks in the suit. If the declarer plays a small spade from the dummy, your partner can let your ♠J win the trick and you still end up taking the first four tricks. We can now complete the rule regarding the lead of an honour card thus:

When we lead an honour card, we promise the honour immediately below it and deny the honour immediately above it. For example, the lead of the ♠Q promises the ♠J but denies the ♠K. If the honour led is the queen, jack or ten, then we may or may not have a higher card in the suit. For example, we would lead the ♠Q from both ♠ Q J 10 and ♠ A Q J. We would lead the ♠J from both ♠ J 10 9 and ♠ K J 10. We would lead the ♠10 from both ♠ 10 9 8 and ♠ Q 10 9 or ♠K 10 9.

Leading the top of an interior sequence also works well in this type of layout:

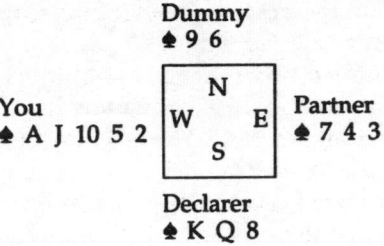

You lead the ♠J and the declarer wins the first trick with the ♠Q. If your partner gets the lead, he can lead back a spade trapping the declarer's remaining ♠K. The defence ends up with four spade tricks.

A broken sequence is one in which you are missing the second or third card in what would otherwise be a four-card or longer sequence. You lead the top of the touching cards to prevent the declarer from getting a cheap trick. You hope that if the declarer has the missing card in the sequence, you will be able to trap it. For example:

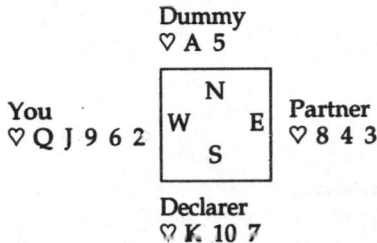

If you were to lead a small heart, the declarer would win the first trick with the ♡10 and end up with three tricks in the suit. By leading the ♡Q, you retain the option to trap the declarer's ♡10 in the above situation. The declarer can win the first trick with the dummy's ♡A, keeping the ♡K and ♡10 in his hand but if your partner gets the lead for the defence, he can lead a heart through the declarer's strength, trapping the ♡10.

Finally, let's review why you lead a low card when you do not have a strong sequence. One reason is to ensure that, if your partner has a high card, you start by playing the high card from the short side first:

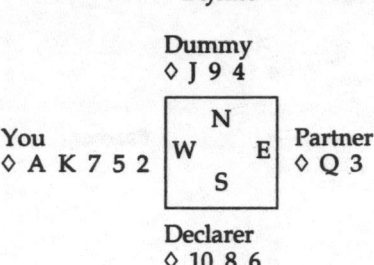

Dummy
◊ J 9 4

You
◊ A K 7 5 2

Partner
◊ Q 3

Declarer
◊ 10 8 6

Leading a low diamond lets the defenders take the first four tricks. If you start with a high diamond, the suit becomes blocked. Worse, if you play both the ◊A and ◊K, your partner's ◊Q never takes a trick and the declarer gets an undeserved trick with the ◊J.

Leading low also helps to preserve communications between the defenders' hands in this type of layout:

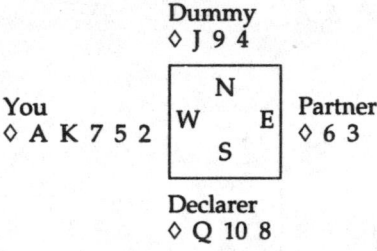

Dummy
◊ J 9 4

You
◊ A K 7 5 2

Partner
◊ 6 3

Declarer
◊ Q 10 8

By leading a low diamond, you ensure that you have an entry back to your winners if your partner subsequently wins a trick. If you started with your high diamonds and then another diamond to establish your small cards, your remaining winners would be stranded since your partner has no diamonds left.

You might hear bridge players giving the advice: "Lead the fourth highest of your longest and strongest suit against a no-trump contract."

For example, from a suit such as ♡ A Q 8 6 2, you would lead the ♡6, fourth down from the top, rather than the ♡2. This is a conventional way to convey some information to your partner about your length in the suit. It is more important, however, that you understand why you lead a low card, rather than a high card, from such suits.

Putting it into practice

Let's put everything together and see what you would lead from the following hands after the auction has gone:

North	East	South	West (You)
	1◊	1NT	Pass
3NT	Pass	Pass	Pass

1	♠ QJ85	2	♠ 963	3	♠ Q95
	♡ 9842		♡ Q85		♡ 842
	◊ J6		◊ QJ4		◊ K32
	♣ 1053		♣ 10653		♣ 9864

Your partner has bid diamonds so, with nothing better to do, you should lead his suit on each of the hands. On the first hand, you lead the ◊J, top of your doubleton. On the second hand, lead the ◊Q, top of your touching high cards. On the last hand, lead the ◊2, low from three or more cards with no touching high cards.

Now, let's see what you would lead in each of the following hands after the auction has gone:

North	East	South	West (You)
	Pass	1NT	Pass
3NT	Pass	Pass	Pass

1	♠ QJ107	2	♠ K4	3	♠ 952
	♡ J863		♡ 983		♡ AJ853
	◊ A7		◊ A10985		◊ J72
	♣ 1084		♣ 742		♣ 94

This time, you have nothing much to go on from the auction, so you will have to look toward your own long suits. On the first hand, you have four cards in both spades and hearts. With a choice, pick the stronger suit. Since you have a sequence, lead the top card, the ♠Q. With the second hand, the diamond suit clearly represents your best chance to develop tricks. Start with the ◊10, top of your interior sequence. On the last hand, you are going to try to develop tricks from your long heart suit. With no sequence to lead from, start with a low heart. Traditionally, you would lead the ♡5, fourth highest.

Summary

When leading against a no-trump contract, always stop to review the bidding before choosing the suit to lead. Use the following guidelines:

- Lead your partner's suit
- Avoid leading a suit bid by the opponents
- Lead your longest suit. With a choice of suits, lead the stronger suit

Having chosen the suit, you must think about the best card to lead. Use the following guidelines:

When leading your partner's suit:
- Lead the top of a doubleton (9 2, Q 3)
- Lead the top of touching high cards (Q J 8, J 10 9)
- Otherwise, lead low (Q 7 2, K 8 4 3)

When leading your own suit:
- Lead the top of a three-card or longer sequence (K Q J 7, Q J 10 8 2)
- Lead the top of an interior sequence (K J 10 9, A 10 9 8 5)
- Lead the top of a broken sequence (K Q 10 8, Q J 9 6 2)
- Otherwise, lead low (fourth best) (K J 8 5, A 10 8 4 3)

Over Zia's shoulder

Hand 1 Dealer: West

North	East	South	West (Zia)
			Pass
Pass	1♠	1NT	Pass
2NT	Pass	3NT	Pass
Pass	Pass		

(Zia)
♠ 9 2
♡ Q 10 9 8 7 3
◇ 5 2
♣ 10 9 8

Luckily, my partner had enough strength to open the bidding. With this motley collection of cards, I was expecting the opponents to reach slam. Looking at the nice interior sequence in hearts, what am I going to lead?

Solution to Hand 1:

Contract: 3NT

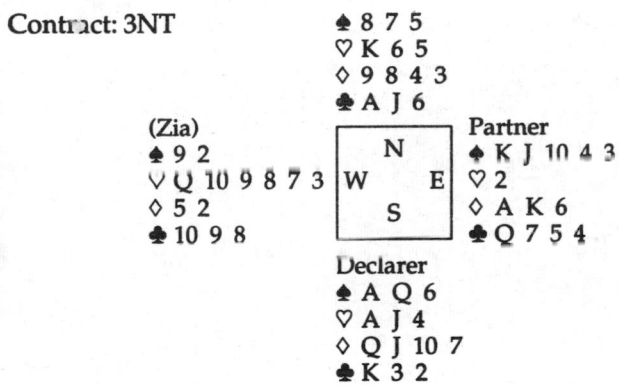

♠ 8 7 5
♡ K 6 5
◇ 9 8 4 3
♣ A J 6

(Zia)
♠ 9 2
♡ Q 10 9 8 7 3
◇ 5 2
♣ 10 9 8

Partner
♠ K J 10 4 3
♡ 2
◇ A K 6
♣ Q 7 5 4

Declarer
♠ A Q 6
♡ A J 4
◇ Q J 10 7
♣ K 3 2

S It's time to stop and review the bidding. My partner has given us a clue what to do by opening the bidding 1♠.

T In thinking about the best card to lead, I am tempted to start with my long heart suit. My partner's suit takes preference, however. I have no reason to believe that my suit is any better than my partner's and, even if I can promote some winners, I have no entry back to my hand to help me take them.

O There's no time to waste. I have to lead my partner's suit right away to avoid giving the declarer the opportunity to establish his suits. Since I am leading my partner's suit, I start with the ♠9, top of a doubleton.

P The defenders' plan springs into action. Leading a spade helps my partner drive out one of the declarer's high spades. When the declarer leads a diamond to try to establish the tricks he needs, my partner wins and leads another spade to drive out the declarer's remaining high card in the suit. The declarer leads another diamond to establish his suit, but he loses the race. My partner wins and takes his three established spade winners to defeat the contract.

If we had led our own suit, we would not have defeated the contract. Apart from being successful, leading my partner's suit had other advantages. If it worked out badly, at least we have a reasonable excuse. If I had led my own suit and it worked out badly, my partner would have been likely to lose a little of his love for me.

Hand 2 Dealer: North

North	East	South	West
			(Zia)
Pass	Pass	2NT	Pass
3NT	Pass	Pass	Pass

```
          (Zia)      ┌──────────┐
          ♠ A Q 9 8 4 │    N     │
          ♡ J 4 2     │ W      E │
          ◇ 9 4       │    S     │
          ♣ 9 7 5     └──────────┘
```

At least I know which suit I'm going to lead against this contract, but which card should I lead? A high spade or a small one?

Solution to Hand 2:

Contract: 3NT

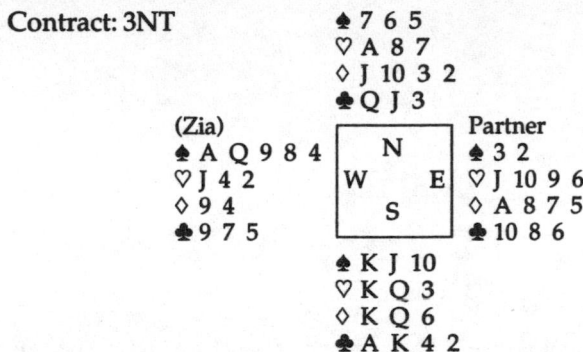

```
                    ♠ 7 6 5
                    ♡ A 8 7
                    ◊ J 10 3 2
                    ♣ Q J 3
   (Zia)         ┌──────────┐    Partner
   ♠ A Q 9 8 4   │    N     │    ♠ 3 2
   ♡ J 4 2       │ W     E  │    ♡ J 10 9 6
   ◊ 9 4         │    S     │    ◊ A 8 7 5
   ♣ 9 7 5       └──────────┘    ♣ 10 8 6
                    ♠ K J 10
                    ♡ K Q 3
                    ◊ K Q 6
                    ♣ A K 4 2
```

S The auction has not given us much to go on, but we are going to have to find five tricks to defeat it.

T With only one sure trick in spades, we'll have to try to establish some tricks through length.

O We may have to give up a spade trick or two to the declarer in order to establish the suit. Is it better to take the ♠A and then drive out the declarer's remaining spade(s), or should we start with a low spade? With no other entries to our hand outside the spade suit, we should start with a low spade. We need to have a strong sequence to lead a high spade.

P We lead the ♠8, fourth highest, and the declarer wins the first trick with the ♠10. This looks a little discouraging, but it's not all over yet. He can take three heart tricks and four club tricks but, sooner or later, he is going to have to lead a diamond to establish his ninth trick. When he does, our partner wins the ◊A and leads back to a spade, trapping the declarer's ♠K and allowing us to take four spade tricks to defeat the contract.

Leading a small spade is the only thing that works on this hand. If we lead another suit, or start with the ♣A, the declarer has an easy time making the contract.

CHAPTER 8

The Use of Trumps in Defence

We often wonder what it would be like to play a sport against the best in the world. At a bridge tournament, you often get the privilege of that experience. There are events which are open and if you want the challenge, you can play a few hands against a player like Omar Sharif.

Defending against a suit contract is, in many ways, similar to defending against a no-trump contract. Against no-trump contracts you can get the extra tricks you need through promotion, through establishing your small cards in long suits and through the finesse. All of these methods can also be used when defending against a trump contract but, because of the trump suit, there are some additional considerations.

Promoting tricks

Promoting winners by driving out a declarer's higher cards is still an excellent source of extra tricks when defending a trump contract, but you may find that you cannot establish as many tricks as you would like because of the declarer's ability to use his trumps once he becomes void in a suit. For example, consider this layout of the spade suit when defending a contract in which hearts are trumps:

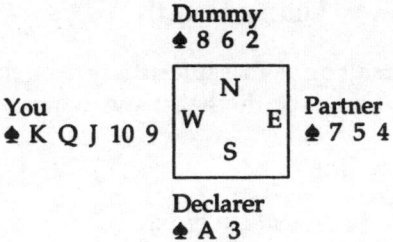

Dummy
♠ 8 6 2

You
♠ K Q J 10 9

Partner
♠ 7 5 4

Declarer
♠ A 3

You lead the ♠K and drive out the declarer's ♠A. If you were defending a no trumps contract, you would now have established four sure tricks for the defence once you regain the lead. In a heart contract, however, you have only established one sure trick since, when you lead the suit a third time, the declarer will be able to *ruff* (trump) with a small trump.

On top of that, you cannot even see how many spades the declarer has left when he wins the first trick with the ♠A. He might have started with only the singleton ♠A, in which case you have no sure tricks to take, or he might have started with three spades, in which case you have two sure tricks to take. The only thing you have to guide you is the bidding and, as we shall discuss in a later chapter, your partner's signals. For example, if the opener has described a balanced hand during the auction, he is unlikely to have a singleton spade. You can be more confident of the number of tricks you have to take when you see the shortness in the dummy.

Using length

Establishing your small cards in a suit suffers from the same problem. Consider this layout of the heart suit when diamonds are trumps:

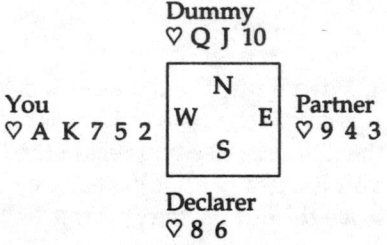

Dummy
♡ Q J 10

You
♡ A K 7 5 2

Partner
♡ 9 4 3

Declarer
♡ 8 6

Defending a no-trump contract, you would probably start by leading a small heart. The dummy would win the first trick but the defence is now poised to take four tricks in the suit when they regain the lead: the ♡A and ♡K and the remaining two long hearts in your hand. This would not work well against a diamond contract, however. Even if you establish your little hearts as winners, the declarer will be able to ruff them with diamonds unless he has run out of trumps. Worse, if you start off by leading a low heart, the declarer will win the first trick and you will not even get both your ♡A and ♡K because the declarer can trump the third round of the suit.

Such considerations mean that you may have to consider different tactics when you lead against a suit contract from those when you lead against a no-trump contract. That is not to say that developing tricks in a long suit is never of any use against a trump contract. After all, the declarer may run out of trumps; then you will be able to take your winners when you regain the lead. In that type of situation, the declarer is said to have *lost control of the hand*. That is, he is no longer capable of stopping you from taking all your winners. We shall see an example of this later in the chapter.

Using the finesse

The defensive finesse works in a suit contract in the same manner as in a no-trump contract. Once again, however, the presence of the trump suit may limit the number of tricks you can get through this technique. Consider this layout of the diamond suit when spades are trumps:

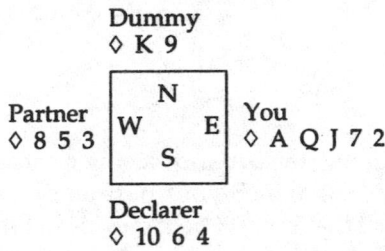

Your partner leads a diamond and you have the dummy's ◊K trapped. That would be great in a no-trump contract, since you would get five tricks in the suit. With spades as trumps, however, the dummy will be able to trump the third round of the suit, limiting you to two tricks. Even if the dummy has no trumps left, the declarer will be able to trump the fourth round of the suit.

Limiting the numbers of winners the defence can take in such suits is, of course, the major reason why your opponents have chosen to play in a trump contract, rather than no trumps. That does not mean that the defence is powerless, however. The declarer's weapon of the trump suit can often be turned against him through resourceful defence.

Giving your partner a ruff

While the declarer can ruff your winners when he runs out of the suit, the defenders can also trump the declarer's winners when they are short in a suit. That is the reason that the declarer usually wants to draw trumps when he has the opportunity, but the defenders may not always give him that chance. Let's look at the following hand where the declarer is in a contract of 4♠ and you start off by leading the ◊A:

Contract: 4♠

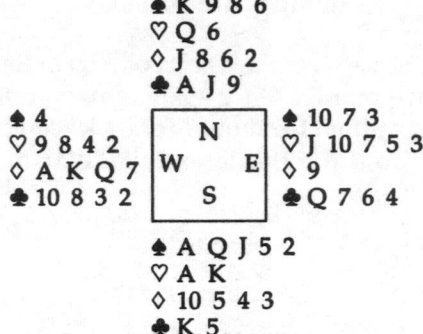

```
                    ♠ K 9 8 6
                    ♡ Q 6
                    ◊ J 8 6 2
                    ♣ A J 9
  ♠ 4                            ♠ 10 7 3
  ♡ 9 8 4 2          N           ♡ J 10 7 5 3
  ◊ A K Q 7      W       E       ◊ 9
  ♣ 10 8 3 2         S           ♣ Q 7 6 4
                    ♠ A Q J 5 2
                    ♡ A K
                    ◊ 10 5 4 3
                    ♣ K 5
```

You start off winning the ◊A and, seeing no reason to switch, continue with the ◊K on which your partner discards a small heart. The way to defeat the contract becomes clear. Since there are exactly thirteen cards in the diamond suit, you can work out that the declarer started with four of them when your partner *shows out* (discards) on the second round. You continue by leading the ◊Q. This would not be such a good idea against a no-trump contract, since it establishes the dummy's ◊J as a winner. Against a suit contract, however, that is only temporary. Following your plan, you lead yet another diamond and your partner is able to defeat the contract by trumping with a small spade.

Defending this contract, it turned out to the defenders' advantage that spades were the trump suit. The declarer was unfortunate that the diamonds were so badly divided but, as a defender, you have to take advantage of such opportunities.

Although the declarer can use his trumps when he becomes void in a suit, that may do him no good if one of the defenders is also void in the suit. Look at how the defenders can co-operate on this hand, defending a contract of 4♠:

Contract: 4♠

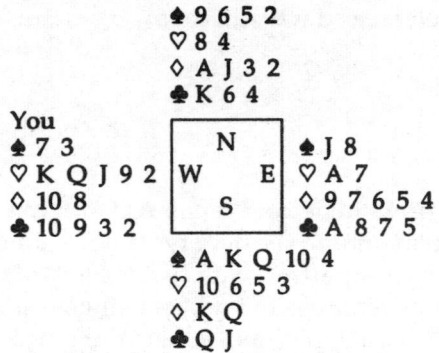

```
                    ♠ 9 6 5 2
                    ♡ 8 4
                    ◇ A J 3 2
                    ♣ K 6 4
You
♠ 7 3                   N            ♠ J 8
♡ K Q J 9 2     W         E         ♡ A 7
◇ 10 8                  S            ◇ 9 7 6 5 4
♣ 10 9 3 2                           ♣ A 8 7 5
                    ♠ A K Q 10 4
                    ♡ 10 6 5 3
                    ◇ K Q
                    ♣ Q J
```

As West, you start off by leading the ♡K, hoping to promote winners in the suit. When the dummy comes down, however, you see that there are only two hearts and that limits the number of tricks you can take in the suit. All is not lost, though, because your partner also has only two hearts. Remembering the earlier discussions about unblocking suits, your partner carefully overtakes your ♡K with the ♡A and returns the suit. When you win the second heart trick, you have to ask yourself the meaning of this sequence of plays by your partner. When you draw the conclusion that your partner must also have a doubleton heart, the defence becomes clearer. You lead another heart. Although the declarer can trump with one of dummy's spades, your partner can *overtrump* with a higher spade. Your partner now takes the ♣A to defeat the contract.

Getting a ruff

Besides looking for opportunities for helping your partner use his trumps against the declarer, you can deliberately set out to try to obtain a ruff. You do this by leading a *short suit*, a singleton or doubleton. Let's see how this works when the auction has gone:

North	East	South	West
			(You)
1NT	Pass	3♠	Pass
4♠	Pass	Pass	Pass

You find yourself on lead with the following hand:

♠ A 8 2
♡ 3
◊ A 6 5 4
♣ J 6 4 3 2

You need four tricks to defeat the contract and can see only two, the ♠A and ◊A (assuming the declarer is not void in diamonds). You might find your partner with two high cards that can win tricks, but a better chance is to lead your singleton heart. You are hoping for one of two things. Either that your partner may be able to win the first heart trick and lead another heart for you to ruff. Or that the declarer will win the first trick but, when you regain the lead with the ♠A, that you will be able to find an entry to your partner's hand, perhaps the ◊K or ♣A, and he can lead a heart for you to trump. Here's the complete layout:

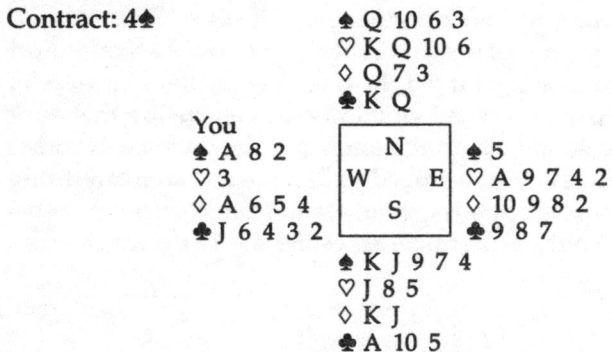

Contract: 4♠

```
                    ♠ Q 10 6 3
                    ♡ K Q 10 6
                    ◊ Q 7 3
                    ♣ K Q
You
♠ A 8 2          N         ♠ 5
♡ 3         W         E    ♡ A 9 7 4 2
◊ A 6 5 4        S         ◊ 10 9 8 2
♣ J 6 4 3 2                ♣ 9 8 7
                    ♠ K J 9 7 4
                    ♡ J 8 5
                    ◊ K J
                    ♣ A 10 5
```

Your heart lead defeats the contract right away. Your partner wins the first trick with the ♡A and leads one back for you to trump. The ♠A and ◊A provide the setting tricks.

Of course, there is a big assumption implicit in the above defence. Your partner must co-operate with your plan by winning the first trick and leading back the suit, even though he can see the heart winners in the dummy. That means that your partner (or you, if you were in partner's place) must be aware of the possibility that you have led a short suit in such a situation. In Chapter 11 we will look at additional ways in which the defenders can help each other when trying to get ruffs.

Running the declarer out of trumps

Earlier in the chapter, we mentioned the possibility of the declarer losing control of the hand, that is, running out of trumps. The defenders can often help bring about the declarer's demise. Look at this hand where you are West:

Contract: 4♠

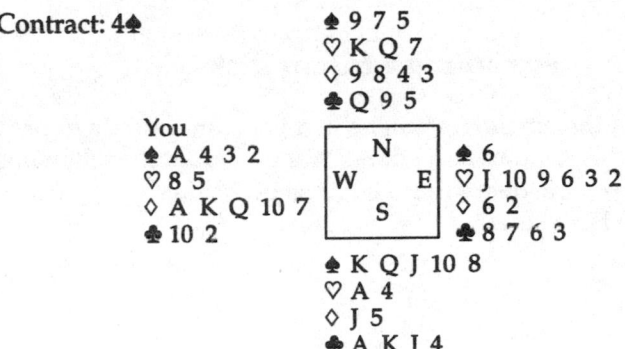

```
                    ♠ 9 7 5
                    ♡ K Q 7
                    ◊ 9 8 4 3
                    ♣ Q 9 5
You
♠ A 4 3 2       N          ♠ 6
♡ 8 5       W       E       ♡ J 10 9 6 3 2
◊ A K Q 10 7     S          ◊ 6 2
♣ 10 2                      ♣ 8 7 6 3
                    ♠ K Q J 10 8
                    ♡ A 4
                    ◊ J 5
                    ♣ A K J 4
```

Looking at the ♠A and potentially three sure tricks in diamonds, you start off by leading the ◊A, ◊K and ◊Q. Unfortunately, the declarer has only a doubleton diamond and is able to trump the third round. The declarer now starts to draw trumps. He has to do this, otherwise you will be able to ruff one of his winners with a small trump. When you win the ♠A, you will have to reconsider your original plan.

Although the declarer was able to trump the third diamond, that brought him down to four trumps, the same number you have. By leading another of your diamond winners, even though you know that the declarer can trump it, you can defeat the contract. When the declarer trumps, he now has fewer trumps left than you do. If he plays the rest of his trumps, he will lose control since you will still have a trump left, along with another diamond winner to take. If the declarer does not draw your trumps but starts playing his winners instead, you will be able to trump one of them and again defeat the contract.

As a general guideline, it does not usually do the defence any harm to make the declarer ruff with the trumps in the longer hand, that is, the hand which holds most of the trumps (usually the declarer's hand). The declarer will probably get tricks with these trumps anyway and you may make him use up his trumps before he is ready. On the other hand, it does not usually do the defence much good to make the declarer trump in the shorter hand (usually the dummy), since the declarer will still have trumps left in the long hand with which to draw trumps and keep control of the hand.

Promoting a trump trick

Occasionally, the defenders will be in a position actually to promote one of their trumps as a winner. Take a look at the following hand where you are defending a contract of 4♡ after your partner has overcalled in spades:

Contract: 4♡

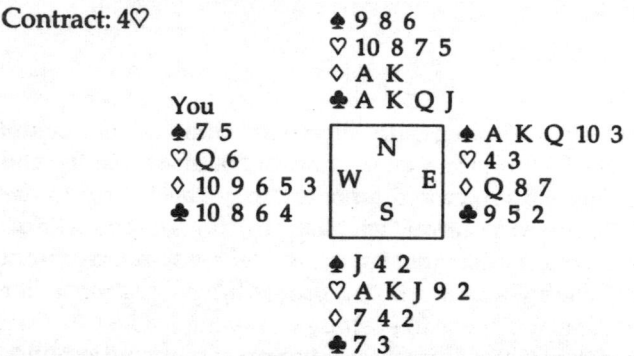

```
                    ♠ 9 8 6
                    ♡ 10 8 7 5
                    ◊ A K
                    ♣ A K Q J
         You
         ♠ 7 5                        ♠ A K Q 10 3
         ♡ Q 6           N            ♡ 4 3
         ◊ 10 9 6 5 3  W     E        ◊ Q 8 7
         ♣ 10 8 6 4       S           ♣ 9 5 2

                    ♠ J 4 2
                    ♡ A K J 9 2
                    ◊ 7 4 2
                    ♣ 7 3
```

You dutifully lead your partner's suit and he takes the first three tricks with the ♠A, ♠K and ♠Q. Where is the defenders' fourth trick going to come from? Your partner can see that there is no hope in the diamond or club suits and he knows that there are no more tricks coming from the spade suit, since everyone else is void. The only hope is in the trump suit. If you have the ♠A or ♠K, you will get a trump trick no matter what your partner does at this point but what if you do not have a natural trump trick, as on the actual hand? Left to his own devices, the declarer will probably play the ♡A and ♡K and you will never get a trick with the ♡Q.

Your partner can help you out by leading another spade, even though he knows that both the declarer and the dummy are void. In most circumstances, it would be a poor idea to lead a suit again when both the declarer and the dummy are void. When the declarer has no losers to get rid of, however, as in the above hand, such a play can sometimes generate a trick for the defence out of thin air.

Look what happens on the actual hand when your partner leads a fourth round of spades. The declarer is lost. If he discards, or trumps with a low heart, you will overruff with your ♡Q to defeat the contract. If he trumps with the ♡A or ♡K, you will discard another suit and your ♡Q has been promoted into the setting trick. This tactic of promoting a trump trick by the defence is called an *uppercut*, since you are effectively delivering a blow to the jaw of the declarer to promote a trump trick for your side. You could not use such a tactic when defending against a no-trump contract so, once again, the defenders do have some special opportunities for creating tricks when the declarer is in a trump contract.

Summary

When defending against a trump contract, the defenders can still use the techniques of promotion, establishing long suits and finessing to develop the extra winners they need. Due to the power of the trump suit, however, they cannot always take all their winners since the declarer can trump them when he runs out of the suit. They will have to take this into consideration when making their plan and when choosing an opening lead.

On the other hand, the defenders have new opportunities when the declarer is playing in a trump suit. They can take advantage of their own shortness in a suit to ruff a declarer's winners. They may also be able to promote winners in the trump suit by running the declarer out of trumps or making use of an *uppercut*.

Over Zia's shoulder

Hand 1 Dealer: South

North	*East*	*South*	*West*
			(Zia)
		1♡	Pass
4♡	Pass	Pass	Pass

West (Zia)

♠ J 6 5 4
♡ K 6 2
◊ 9 8 5 3 2
♣ 4

The opponents have bounced into a game again and I'm going to have to find a lead to set them back on their heels. Where does my best chance lie?

Solution to Hand 1:

Contract: 4♡

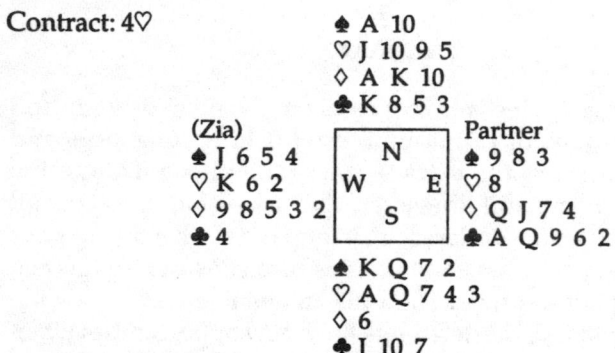

```
              ♠ A 10
              ♡ J 10 9 5
              ◊ A K 10
              ♣ K 8 5 3
(Zia)                        Partner
♠ J 6 5 4      N             ♠ 9 8 3
♡ K 6 2    W       E         ♡ 8
◊ 9 8 5 3 2     S            ◊ Q J 7 4
♣ 4                          ♣ A Q 9 6 2
              ♠ K Q 7 2
              ♡ A Q 7 4 3
              ◊ 6
              ♣ J 10 7
```

S We need four tricks to defeat the opponents' 4♡ contract.

T We do not appear to have any sure tricks in our hand.

O Perhaps I will get a trick with my ♡K if the declarer holds the ♡A, but I will require some help from my partner if we are to defeat the contract. I don't want to ask for any more help than I need, so perhaps I can spot some further potential in my own hand. Since this is a trump contract, I can try leading my single-ton club. If my partner can get the lead, I should be able to get a ruff with one of my little trumps. That way I'll only need a couple of tricks from my partner's hand.

P Leading my singleton club quickly puts paid to the declarer's chances of making the contract. On the actual hand, our lead traps the dummy's ♣K, and my partner is able to win the first two club tricks. When I show out on the second round, discarding one of my small diamonds, my partner has no trouble leading a third round of clubs for me to ruff. I then sit back and wait for my trick with the ♡K.

Perhaps I was lucky to find that my partner had such a nice club holding. Nonetheless, I did help make a little of my own luck by seizing the opportunity to lead a singleton against a trump contract.

Hand 2 Dealer: South

North	East	South	West
			(Zia)
		3♠	4♡
4♠	Pass	Pass	Pass

```
                        Dummy
                        ♠ A K
                        ♡ 6 5
                        ◇ A Q J 3 2
                        ♣ K 5 4 3
        (Zia)
        ♠ Q 2          ┌─────────┐
        ♡ A K Q J 4    │ N       │
        ◇ 9 7 5        │ W     E │
        ♣ A 7 6        │   S     │
                       └─────────┘
```

South's pre-emptive opening bid has got the auction up high pretty quickly. This time, things look a bit better even before I make my opening lead, since it looks as though I have at least three sure tricks and there must be some potential for a trick with my ♠Q. After leading the ♡A, the dummy comes down and I am in a better position to adjust my plan. The declarer plays a small heart from the dummy and both my partner and the declarer follow with small hearts. Where do I go from here?

Solution to Hand 2:

Contract: 4♠

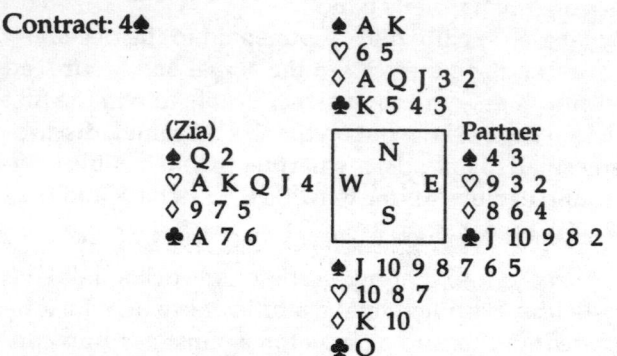

           ♠ A K
           ♡ 6 5
           ◊ A Q J 3 2
           ♣ K 5 4 3

(Zia)
♠ Q 2
♡ A K Q J 4
◊ 9 7 5
♣ A 7 6

Partner
♠ 4 3
♡ 9 3 2
◊ 8 6 4
♣ J 10 9 8 2

           ♠ J 10 9 8 7 6 5
           ♡ 10 8 7
           ◊ K 10
           ♣ Q

S We are going to have to find four tricks to defeat 4♠.

T It looks as though we have three sure tricks, the ♡A, ♡K and ♣A.

O Where can our fourth trick come from? There is some possibility that my partner has the ◊K but, even then, the declarer might have a singleton. If the declarer has three hearts, however, I can promote my ♠Q by forcing him to trump in the dummy.

P Putting my plan into action, I take the ♡A and ♡K and then take my ♣A. I do not want to give the declarer the opportunity to discard a club loser on the dummy's diamonds. Now I apply the coup de grâce and lead the ♡Q. The declarer has no choice. To win the trick, he must ruff with the dummy's ♠K. When he plays the ♠A, my ♠Q has become a winner.

CHAPTER 9

The Opening Lead against a Trump Contract

Even if you don't like cards, bridge may be your game. It is the Rolls-Royce of card games.

Some things do not change regardless of whether you are leading against a trump contract or a no-trump contract. You still want to take enough tricks to defeat the contract. If your partner bids a suit during the auction, it is usually a good idea to lead it. As we saw in Chapter 7, however, the trump suit does have an effect on where the defenders' tricks can come from and we must take this into account when deciding on the best opening lead.

Reviewing the bidding

The first step in selecting an opening lead is to STOP and review the bidding. There are always some clues to be found. Consider the following auction:

North	East	South	West
			(You)
1♣	Pass	1♠	Pass
1NT	Pass	3♡	Pass
4♡	Pass	Pass	Pass

What do we know about North's hand? He should have four clubs for his opening bid of 1♣. His 1NT rebid showed a balanced hand of 15–17 points and, since he did not support his partner's spade suit, he cannot have four of them. On the other hand, he did support the responder's second suit, so he is likely to have four hearts. We can expect the dummy to come down looking something like this:

♠ J4
♡ AJ65
◇ A92
♣ KQ97

What about the declarer's (South's) hand? His first response was 1♠, so he must have at least four of them, and he later bid hearts, so he has at least four of them as well. If he had four hearts and only four spades, he would have responded 1♡, bidding the lower-ranking suit first to make it easier to find a fit in either major suit. Since he bid spades first, the inference is that his spades are longer than his hearts, so he has at least five of them.

South made a forcing rebid by jumping to 3♡, so he must have enough strength to want to be in a game contract opposite the opener's 1NT rebid. The declarer's hand might look something like this:

♠ AQ1062
♡ KQ108
◇ 865
♣ J

Thinking about the best lead

Reviewing the above bidding gives us the help we need to find the best lead with the following hand:

♠ K95
♡ 73
◇ Q1043
♣ 10642

The picture constructed from the bidding steers us towards the diamond suit. Leading a spade is likely to help the declarer rather than the defenders. Hearts is the trump suit, and leading one is likely to help the declarer by starting to draw trumps. The declarer will then have the time to establish his suits. North has bid clubs, so is likely to have some of his high cards there. Leading a club may help the declarer promote winners in the suit. Everything points to leading a diamond. When you lead one, you are amply rewarded when the complete hand turns out to be:

Contract: 4♡

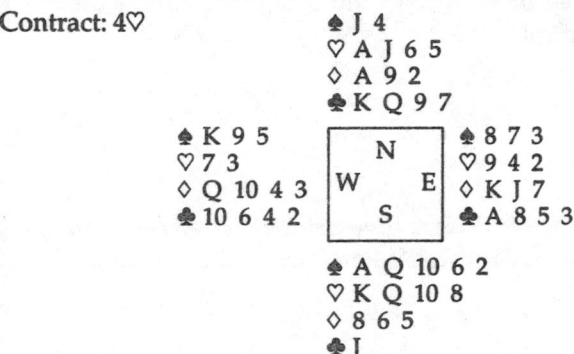

```
                    ♠ J 4
                    ♡ A J 6 5
                    ◇ A 9 2
                    ♣ K Q 9 7
  ♠ K 9 5         ┌─────────┐      ♠ 8 7 3
  ♡ 7 3           │    N    │      ♡ 9 4 2
  ◇ Q 10 4 3      │ W     E │      ◇ K J 7
  ♣ 10 6 4 2      │    S    │      ♣ A 8 5 3
                  └─────────┘
                    ♠ A Q 10 6 2
                    ♡ K Q 10 8
                    ◇ 8 6 5
                    ♣ J
```

On a diamond lead, the defenders are able to promote sure tricks in the suit by driving out the dummy's ◇A. When the declarer plays a club, your partner can win the ♣A and the defenders can take their two diamond tricks. Eventually, you also get a spade trick when the declarer's spade finesse loses. Once again, you have found the only lead to defeat a contract.

Choosing the suit to lead

Against no-trump contracts you were usually looking towards developing tricks in the partnership's longest combined suit. As we saw in Chapter 8, however, establishing winners in a long suit may not do much good when defending against a suit contract because of the declarer's ability to trump once he runs out of a suit. To compensate, you may be able to get tricks from shortness, using your side's trumps to ruff the declarer's winners.

As when leading against no-trump contracts, you should give priority to leading your partner's suit. Your partner is likely to have some strength in the suit he bid and that may be a good source of tricks for the defenders. For example, suppose the auction proceeds this way:

North	East	South	West
			(You)
1NT	2◊	4♠	Pass
Pass	Pass		

You find yourself on lead with the following hand against the declarer's 4♠ contract:

♠ 10 7
♡ 8 7 5 4
◊ J 3 2
♣ J 10 9 8

With no clearly better choice, give priority to leading your partner's suit. This works out well when the complete hand is:

Contract: 4♠

```
                    ♠ A 9 3
                    ♡ J 10 9 3
                    ◊ K 4
                    ♣ A 7 6 5
    You         ┌──────────┐
    ♠ 10 7      │    N     │    ♠ 6 2
    ♡ 8 7 5 4   │ W     E  │    ♡ A K 2
    ◊ J 3 2     │    S     │    ◊ A Q 10 9 8 6
    ♣ J 10 9 6  └──────────┘    ♣ 4 3
                    ♠ K Q J 8 5 4
                    ♡ Q 6
                    ◊ 7 5
                    ♣ K Q 2
```

When you lead a diamond, the dummy's ◊K is trapped. Your partner can take the first two diamond tricks and also the ♡A and ♡K to defeat the contract. If you were to lead another suit, the top of your club sequence perhaps, the declarer would make the contract. The declarer can win the club lead and, after drawing trumps, can promote the dummy's hearts into winners by driving out your partner's high hearts. Each time your partner wins a heart trick, he cannot lead diamonds without giving a trick to the dummy's ◊K. Eventually, the declarer will be able to discard one or both of his small diamonds on the dummy's extra heart winners.

As when leading against no-trump contracts, you generally want to avoid leading a suit bid by one of the opponents. They are likely to have some strength in the suit and you will probably be helping the declarer, rather than hurting him. For example, consider this suit layout where the declarer has bid diamonds during the auction:

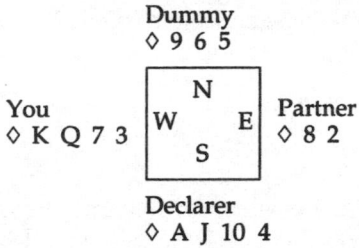

Leading the ◊K will promote your ◊Q as a trick for the defence but, after the declarer has drawn trumps, he will be able to promote the rest of his diamond suit into winners. If you left the declarer to play the suit himself, you would end up with two tricks instead of one.

When choosing one of your own suits to lead, prefer a suit in which you have a strong sequence to leading a low card from a suit in which you have one or two high cards. For example, consider this layout of the club suit in a contract in which diamonds are trumps:

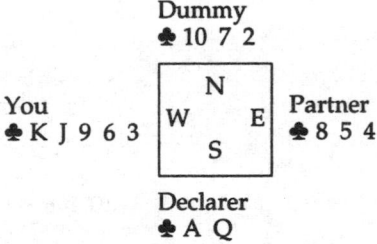

Against a no-trump contract, it might be a good idea to lead a small card from this suit. Although the declarer can win the first trick with the ♣Q, you can lead the suit again when you regain the lead to drive out the declarer's ♣A and establish three winners in the suit. Against a suit contract, however, a small club lead might prove fatal. The declarer wins the first trick with the ♣Q and the second with the ♣A. You now have some winners in the suit but, when you lead one, the declarer will be able to trump it. Instead of getting three tricks in the suit, you end up with none. It is better to lead another suit and wait until your partner or the declarer leads a club. That way, at least you get one trick with your ♣K.

Here is an example in a complete hand. The auction is as follows:

North	East	South	West
			(You)
Pass	Pass	1♡	Pass
2♡	Pass	4♡	Pass
Pass	Pass		

You have to lead from this hand:

♠ KQJ
♡ 97
♦ KJ982
♣ 654

With a choice of suits to lead and no help from your partner, the ♠K is a better choice than a diamond or one of the other suits. You can see that leading the ♠K is likely to promote two winners for the defence. Who knows what will happen if you lead a diamond? Here is the complete hand:

Contract: 4♡

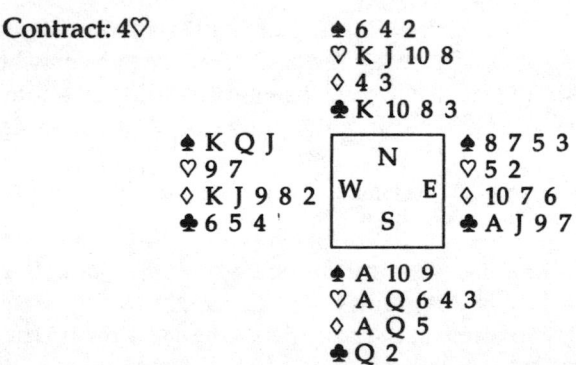

♠ 6 4 2
♡ K J 10 8
♦ 4 3
♣ K 10 8 3

♠ K Q J   ♠ 8 7 5 3
♡ 9 7   ♡ 5 2
♦ K J 9 8 2   ♦ 10 7 6
♣ 6 5 4   ♣ A J 9 7

♠ A 10 9
♡ A Q 6 4 3
♦ A Q 5
♣ Q 2

When you lead the ♠K, the defence has no trouble defeating the contract. You promote two sure tricks and eventually get tricks from your partner's ♣A and your ◊K. If you had led a diamond, the declarer would never have to lose a trick in the suit. He would win the first trick with his ◊Q, take the ◊A and trump his remaining small diamond with one of the dummy's trumps.

It is especially dangerous to lead a low card when you hold the ace of a suit. Consider this layout of the diamond suit when hearts are trumps:

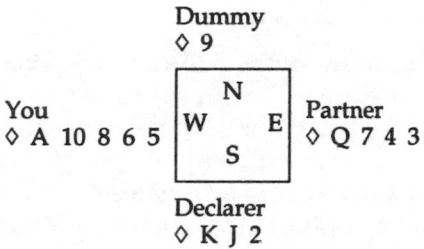

Leading a low diamond might work well against a no-trump contract. After the declarer wins the first trick, your partner may get the lead and lead a diamond through the declarer trapping the declarer's remaining high card. Against a suit contract, it is unlikely to work very well. The declarer will win the first trick and be able to trump his remaining diamonds in the dummy. You do not even take a trick with your ◊A. If you do decide to lead a suit in which you have the ace, you are usually better off leading the ace than leading a small card.

As we saw in Chapter 8, leading a short suit is an alternative worth considering against a trump contract. Your partner may be able to win a trick and give you a ruff. Here is an example in a complete hand where you have to find an opening lead against a 4♠ contract:

Contract: 4♠
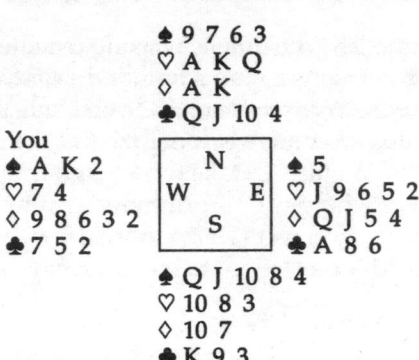

```
                        ♠ 9 7 6 3
                        ♡ A K Q
                        ◇ A K
                        ♣ Q J 10 4
You
♠ A K 2          ┌─────────┐          ♠ 5
♡ 7 4            │   N     │          ♡ J 9 6 5 2
◇ 9 8 6 3 2      │ W   E   │          ◇ Q J 5 4
♣ 7 5 2          │   S     │          ♣ A 8 6
                 └─────────┘
                        ♠ Q J 10 8 4
                        ♡ 10 8 3
                        ◇ 10 7
                        ♣ K 9 3
```

With nothing much in any of the side suits, you visualize the possibility of getting an extra trick with your small spade. To do this, you start by leading a heart. The declarer wins and starts to draw trumps. Winning the first trick with the ♠K, you continue with your plan and lead another heart, making yourself void. The declarer wins and continues to lead trumps. Winning the next trick with the ♠A, you now have one more problem to overcome. You have to get to your partner's hand. The only option appears to be in clubs and, when you lead one, you are fortunate to find your partner with the ♣A. With luck, your partner has been watching your efforts in the heart suit and, realizing what you are up to, leads another heart to give you a ruff and defeat the contract.

Leading a trump

There is one other consideration when defending a trump contract and that is to lead a trump! This may seem to violate the earlier caution about avoiding leading a suit bid by the opponents, but there are a couple of times when, after reviewing the bidding, you can come to the conclusion that it represents the best chance to defeat the contract.

A declarer will often make use of the dummy's trumps to ruff some of the losers in his hand when the dummy is short in a suit. When the auction indicates that this might be the case, leading trumps at every opportunity may thwart the declarer's plan. We will look at an example of preventing the declarer from using the dummy's trumps in Chapter 12.

The other time to lead a trump is when it appears dangerous to lead anything else. This is called a *passive defence*. You try not to give up a trick on the opening lead and you leave the declarer to fend for himself. For example, consider the following auction:

North	East	South	West
			(You)
1♣	Pass	1♡	Pass
2NT	Pass	3♠	Pass
4♠	Pass	Pass	Pass

You are on lead with this hand:

♠ 7 6 4
♡ Q 10 9 6
◇ A 9 5
♣ Q 10 7

Everything looks dangerous. The opponents have bid spades, hearts and clubs and you want to avoid leading the ◇A since it may promote the ◇K in either the declarer or the dummy's hand. This is the time to go passive and lead a spade. Here is the complete hand:

Contract: 4♠

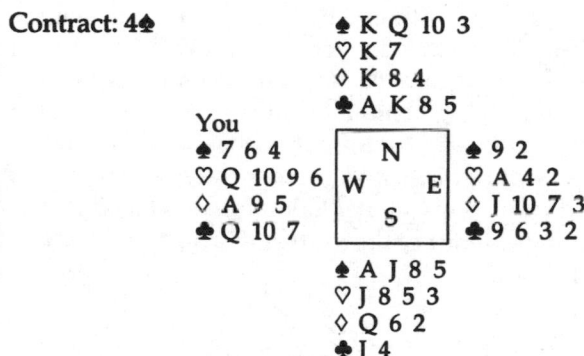

```
                    ♠ K Q 10 3
                    ♡ K 7
                    ◇ K 8 4
                    ♣ A K 8 5
      You
      ♠ 7 6 4          N          ♠ 9 2
      ♡ Q 10 9 6   W     E        ♡ A 4 2
      ◇ A 9 5          S          ◇ J 10 7 3
      ♣ Q 10 7                    ♣ 9 6 3 2
                    ♠ A J 8 5
                    ♡ J 8 5 3
                    ◇ Q 6 2
                    ♣ J 4
```

The trump lead gives nothing away. Left to his own devices, the declarer loses two heart tricks and two diamond tricks. If you had led a heart, the declarer might make the contract by playing a small heart from the dummy, forcing your partner to win with the ♡A and establishing the dummy's ♡K as a trick. If you had led the

◊A, you would have promoted both the ◊K and ◊Q into tricks. If you had led a club, the declarer could play a small club from the dummy and win the first trick with the ♣J, then use the dummy's extra club winner to discard one of his diamond losers.

Choosing the card to lead

Having selected the suit you are going to lead, you must choose the specific card in the suit. The guidelines are virtually identical to those when leading a suit against a no-trump contract:

When leading partner's suit:
- Lead the top of a doubleton (9 2, Q 3)
- Lead the top of touching high cards (Q J 8, J 10 9)
- Otherwise, lead low* (Q 7 2, K 8 4 3)

When leading your own suit:
- Lead the top of a two-card or longer sequence (K Q 8 7, Q J 10 2)
- Lead the top of an interior sequence* (K J 10 9, Q 10 9 5)
- Lead the top of a broken sequence (K Q 10 8, Q J 9 6 2)
- Otherwise, lead low* (fourth best) (K J 8 5, Q 10 8 4 3)

We have already discussed the reason why you avoid leading a low card against a trump contract when you hold the ace of the suit you are leading. There is a danger that you will never get a trick with your ace if the declarer or the dummy holds a singleton.

Let's look at the reasoning behind the other small change. That is, that you would usually lead the top of two touching cards when leading your own suit against a trump contract, whereas you would tend to lead low from a similar holding against a no-trump contract. Consider this layout of the heart suit in a contract where spades are the trump suit:

---

* Except when holding the ace, in which case you should lead it.

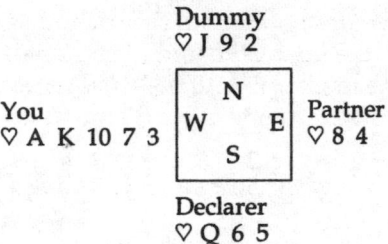

You would lead a low heart against a no-trump contract so that your partner would have a heart left as an entry back to your hand if he gets the lead. That gives you the best chance of taking four tricks in the suit. If spades are trumps, however, it is unlikely to do much good to try to develop your small hearts into winners. By leading the ♡A and ♡K, you guarantee two tricks in the suit and, on the actual layout, you can lead the suit again and your partner will be able to trump the declarer's winner with a small spade, giving the defence a third trick.

Here is another possible layout for the heart suit when defending against a trump contract:

<table>
<tr><td></td><td>Dummy
♡ 10 5</td><td></td></tr>
<tr><td>You
♡ K Q 8 7 4</td><td>N
W   E
S</td><td>Partner
♡ 9 6 3</td></tr>
<tr><td></td><td>Declarer
♡ A J 2</td><td></td></tr>
</table>

If you lead a small heart, the declarer will end up with no losers in the suit. He can win the first trick with the ♡10 or ♡J, play the ♡A and ruff his remaining heart with one of the dummy's trumps. By leading the ♡K, at least you are sure of promoting one winner in the suit.

Putting it into practice

Let's put the choice of suit and the choice of card together to see what you would lead from the following hands after the auction has gone:

North	East	South	West
			(You)
	1◊	1♡	Pass
3♡	Pass	Pass	Pass

1	♠ QJ85	2	♠ 963	3	♠ J95
	♡ 9842		♡ Q85		♡ 842
	◊ Q3		◊ J104		◊ A32
	♣ 1053		♣ 10653		♣ 9864

Your partner has bid diamonds so, with nothing clearly better to do, you should lead his suit on each hand.

On the first hand, lead the ◊Q, top of your doubleton.

On the second hand, you would lead the ◊J, top of your touching high cards.

On the last hand, you would lead the ◊2, low from three or more cards against a no-trump contract. Against a suit contract, however, you should not usually lead a small card when you have the ace. Lead the ◊A.

Now, let's see what you would lead on the following hands after the auction has gone:

North	East	South	West
			(You)
	Pass	1♠	Pass
3♠	Pass	4♠	Pass
Pass	Pass		

1	♠ Q107	2	♠ 842	3	♠ 952
	♡ KJ83		♡ 98632		♡ AQ53
	◊ QJ107		◊ 8		◊ K72
	♣ J8		♣ J432		♣ Q94

This time, you do not have any help from your partner, so you will have to look towards your own suits.

On the first hand, you have a strong sequence in diamonds and that is preferable to your heart suit, in which you are missing the ♡A and ♡Q. Lead the ◊Q, top of the touching cards.

On the second hand, you are going to need to find tricks somewhere and the only feature of your hand is the singleton diamond.

Lead it and hope you can get one or more ruffs with your small trumps.

On the last hand, every suit looks dangerous. Lead a low trump, trying not to give anything away with the lead. You might even be able to get rid of enough of the dummy's trumps to stop the declarer from ruffing some of his losers.

Summary

When leading against a trump contract, always stop to review the bidding before choosing the suit to lead. Use the following guidelines:

- Lead your partner's suit
- Avoid leading a suit bid by the opponents
- Lead from a strong sequence, if possible, rather than a suit with only one or two high cards
- Lead from a short suit if you think you can get a ruff
- Lead a trump if everything else looks dangerous. Lead a trump if you think that you can prevent declarer from trumping his losing cards with the dummy's small trumps.

Having chosen the suit, you must think about the best card to lead. Use the following guidelines:

When leading partner's suit:
- Lead the top of a doubleton (9 2, Q 3)
- Lead the top of touching high cards (Q J 8, J 10 9)
- Otherwise, lead low* (Q 7 2, K 8 4 3)

When leading your own suit:
- Lead the top of a two-card or longer sequence (K Q 8 7, Q J 10 2)
- Lead the top of an interior sequence* (K J 10 9, Q 10 9 5)
- Lead the top of a broken sequence (K Q 10 8, Q J 9 6 2)
- Otherwise, lead low* (fourth best) (K J 8 5, Q 10 8 4 3)

* Except when holding the ace, in which case you should lead it.

Over Zia's shoulder

Hand 1 Dealer: South

North	East	South	West
			(Zia)
		1◊	Pass
1♡	Pass	2♣	Pass
3◊	Pass	4♣	Pass
4♡	Pass	5◊	Pass
Pass	Pass		

(Zia)
♠ K J 9 8 6
♡ A 2
◊ 4 3
♣ Q J 10 8

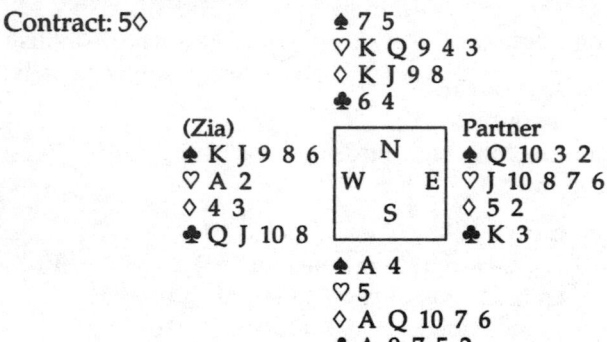

That was quite an auction by the opponents. I have a strong sequence in clubs and a club lead looks less dangerous than a spade – but is it?

Solution to Hand 1:

Contract: 5◊

```
                 ♠ 7 5
                 ♡ K Q 9 4 3
                 ◊ K J 9 8
                 ♣ 6 4
(Zia)                          Partner
♠ K J 9 8 6    N              ♠ Q 10 3 2
♡ A 2        W   E            ♡ J 10 8 7 6
◊ 4 3          S              ◊ 5 2
♣ Q J 10 8                    ♣ K 3
                 ♠ A 4
                 ♡ 5
                 ◊ A Q 10 7 6
                 ♣ A 9 7 5 2
```

S Stop and review the bidding. The opponents have spoken to each other during the bidding conversation, describing their hands. The declarer bid clubs twice, likely showing a five-card suit, so we are more likely to be helping him by leading a club. On the other hand, they avoided playing in 3NT, choosing to play in a minor suit instead. From the auction, it sounds as though they were afraid of the spade suit, since they bid all the other suits. Let's use that information to our advantage and choose a spade.

T Think about the best card to lead. Without touching high cards, we should lead a small spade, traditionally, fourth best. We'll lead the ♠8.

O When the dummy comes down, we can work further on organizing our plan of defence. My partner's (hoped for) ♠Q drives out the declarer's ♠A, promoting my ♠K into a winner. Since the declarer has bid clubs and diamonds and never supported hearts, we expect him to have a singleton. If he leads a heart, we plan to take the ♡A and take our ♠K before the rats get at it. We'll have to hope we can get one more trick from clubs or diamonds.

P Once we put our plan into action, the declarer has no chance. When he wins the first trick with the ♠A and leads his singleton heart towards the dummy, we take the ♡A and the ♠K before the declarer can discard his losing spade on the dummy's hearts. Later in the hand, we get a club trick since the declarer cannot discard all his club losers on the dummy's hearts.

If we had led anything else, the declarer would be able to establish a heart winner in the dummy on which to discard his losing spade.

Hand 2 Dealer: East

North	East	South	West
			(Zia)
	Pass	1♠	Pass
4♠	Pass	4NT	Pass
5♡	Pass	6♠	Pass
Pass	Pass		

(Zia)
♠ 5 4 2
♡ 9
◊ 9 6 5 4
♣ Q 10 8 4 3

```
      N
   W     E
      S
```

If you played as much rubber bridge as I do, you would get used to being on lead with a large amount of money at stake. It hurts when you do the wrong thing – but we won't, will we?

Solution to Hand 2:

Contract: 6♠

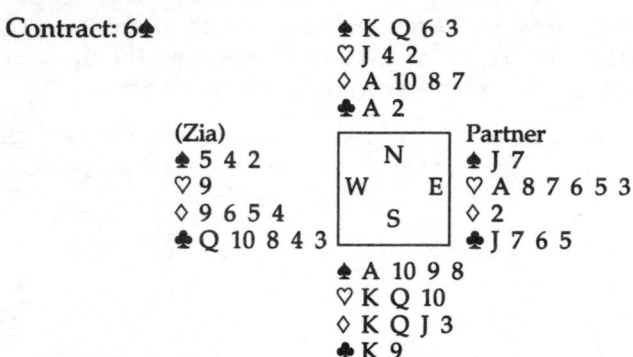

♠ K Q 6 3
♡ J 4 2
◊ A 10 8 7
♣ A 2

(Zia)
♠ 5 4 2
♡ 9
◊ 9 6 5 4
♣ Q 10 8 4 3

Partner
♠ J 7
♡ A 8 7 6 5 3
◊ 2
♣ J 7 6 5

♠ A 10 9 8
♡ K Q 10
◊ K Q J 3
♣ K 9

S We need two tricks and the opponents' direct and rapid auction has not given us much to go on. They have bid a slam, however, so I cannot expect too much from my partner.

T In thinking about the best card to lead, I have the option of leading my singleton heart, hoping my partner has the ♡A and can give me a ruff, or leading a club, hoping my partner has the ♣K and I can promote a trick with my ♣Q.

O My partner will need two high cards to defeat the contract if we lead a club (or a diamond). That is, he will need the ♣K to promote my ♣Q to winning rank, and he will also need another high card to take the second trick for the defence. If I lead a heart, though, I need him to have only one good card – the ♡A or the ♠A. It is a good principle of defence that when you have a choice of plans, you should follow the one which requires least help from your partner. So the best choice appears to to be my singleton heart.

P Putting our plan into action, I lead the ♡9 and find my partner with the one card we need. He wins with the ♡A and has little difficulty figuring out what we are up to. He returns a heart and we take the setting trick with the lowly ♣2.

This hand reminds me of David and Goliath. The opponents had almost all the strength, but our carefully aimed blow defeated the contract.

CHAPTER 10

After Partner Leads

Bridge is the only sport where the participants pay at a tournament and the spectators get in free.

When it is your partner who has made the opening lead, you are able to see his first card and the dummy before you have to STOP and make your plan. You have additional information. You should review the bidding to see what clues you have about the cards in the declarer's hand. Your partner's lead has also told you more about his hand than just the card he chose to lead. For example, if he has led the top of a sequence, you can expect him to have the next lower card but not the next higher card, and so on. Even the first card the declarer plays from the dummy will provide you with a further clue as to your best plan.

Since you will be the third person to play to the first trick, your position is sometimes referred to as *third hand* and this chapter looks at some guidelines for third-hand play. Of course, any time your partner leads to a trick throughout the hand, you will be in the position of third hand and can use the same principles discussed here.

Playing third hand high

As third hand, you are the last player to contribute a card to the trick for your side. Unless your partner's card is clearly going to win the trick, the card you choose to play will be vital in determining which side wins the trick. In general, you want to make your best effort to win the trick for your side, although, as we shall see, sometimes there is more to gain by letting the declarer win the first trick.

When your partner leads a low card that is obviously not going to win the trick, the general principle you follow is *third hand high*. That is, you tend to play as high a card as necessary to try to win the trick. Let's look at an example where your partner has led the ♠2 against a no trumps contract:

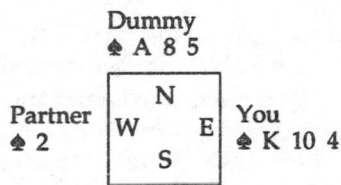

Dummy
♠ A 8 5

Partner   N   You
♠ 2   W   E   ♠ K 10 4
                 S

If the declarer plays the dummy's ♠A on this trick, then there is nothing you can play to win the trick. That does not mean that the card you play is unimportant. As you will see in Chapter 11, the card you choose can convey important information to your partner. For now, let's suppose that the declarer plays the dummy's ♠5. Which card do you play? Being in third hand, you want to try to win the trick for your side and you can do this by playing the ♠K, third hand high. What about playing the ♠10 instead of the ♠K, saving the ♠K for later? The problem with making such a half-hearted effort is that it may cost your side a trick. For example, here is the complete layout of the suit:

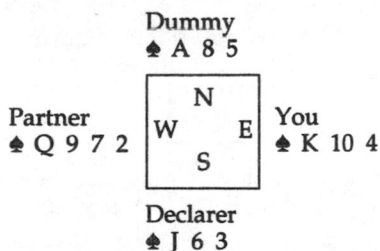

Dummy
♠ A 8 5

Partner   N   You
♠ Q 9 7 2   W   E   ♠ K 10 4
                 S

Declarer
♠ J 6 3

If you play the ♠10, the declarer will win with the ♠J and still have the ♠A left as a second trick in the suit. If you play the ♠K, the declarer only gets one trick. His ♠J is trapped when you return the suit.

Let's change the layout slightly:

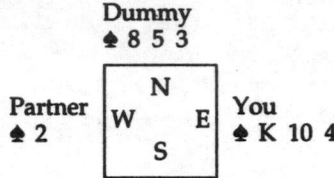

Now it is not so clear that playing the ♠K will win the trick. What if the declarer has the ♠A? Nonetheless, you should put the guideline to work and play the ♠K, third hand high, making your best effort to win the trick. There are a number of possible ways in which the missing high cards might be distributed. Let's start with an example where your partner holds the ♠A:

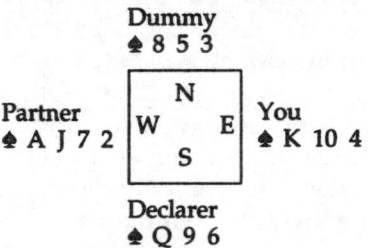

If you feebly play the ♠10, the declarer will win a trick with the ♠Q. Whereas, if you play the ♠K, you will win the trick and can lead back a spade to trap the declarer's ♠Q. The declarer ends up with no tricks in the suit. Now let's give the declarer the ♠A:

Dummy
♠ 8 5 3

Partner
♠ Q 9 7 2

You
♠ K 10 4

Declarer
♠ A J 6

If you play the ♠10, the declarer wins the ♠J and ends up with two tricks in the suit. Playing the ♠K does not actually win the trick, but it drives out the declarer's ♠A, promoting your partner's ♠Q into a winner. Better still, if you regain the lead, you can lead another spade, trapping the declarer's ♠J and giving your side three tricks in the suit.

Playing only as high as necessary

You do not have to play your highest card in third hand, only as high as necessary to make your best effort to win the trick. Look at this layout where your partner has led the ♡3:

```
            Dummy
            ♡ 8 6 4
              ┌─────────┐
              │    N    │
    Partner   │ W     E │  You
    ♡ 3       │    S    │  ♡ Q J 2
              └─────────┘
```

When the declarer plays a small heart from the dummy, your ♡Q and ♡J have equal value. Either one of them could be used to drive out any high card the declarer might hold. In such situations, you should play the *lower* card, the ♡J. What difference does it make? Let's look at the complete layout from your partner's perspective:

```
            Dummy
            ♡ 8 6 4
              ┌─────────┐
              │    N    │
    Partner   │ W     E │  You
    ♡ K 9 5 3 │    S    │  ♡ Q J 2
              └─────────┘
            Declarer
            ♡ A 10 7
```

When your ♡J drives out the declarer's ♡A, your partner is able to work out that you must hold the ♡Q as well. If the declarer held the ♡Q, he would have won the first trick with it, keeping his ♡A as a second trick in the suit. If your partner regains the lead, he can confidently lead another small heart to your ♡Q and you could lead your last heart back to his remaining winners.

If you were to play the ♡Q, your partner will assume that the complete layout is something like this:

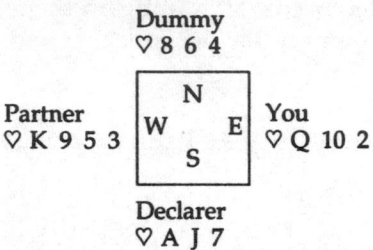

Dummy
♡ 8 6 4

Partner
♡ K 9 5 3

You
♡ Q 10 2

Declarer
♡ A J 7

If he regains the lead, he will not want to lead another small heart since he would expect that the declarer would be able to win it with the ♡J.

Playing the lower of touching cards when playing third hand high has a similar effect to leading the top of touching cards. It can help your partner to visualize the location of cards he cannot actually see.

Finessing against the dummy

Suppose your partner leads the ◊4 in this layout:

Dummy
◊ Q 8 3

Partner
◊ 4

You
◊ K J 2

When the declarer plays a small diamond from the dummy, you would play the ◊J, not the ◊K, since the ◊J is as high as necessary to try to win the trick. The complete layout might be:

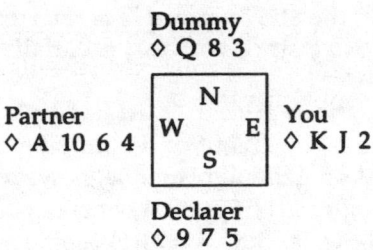

Playing the ◊J allows the defenders to take the first four tricks in the suit. If you were to play the ◊K on the first trick, the declarer would eventually get a trick with the dummy's ◊Q. Playing only as high a card as necessary in third hand is not always straightforward. Let's change the situation slightly:

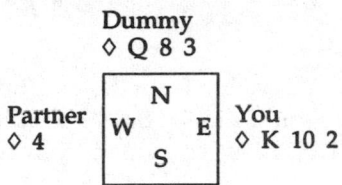

When your partner leads the ◊4 and the declarer plays the ◊3 from the dummy, should you play the ◊K or the ◊10? How high is it necessary to play? The situation is essentially equivalent to the previous layout but it is much more difficult to visualize when you do not have the ◊J. Let's look at the complete layout:

```
              Dummy
              ◊ Q 8 3
                 N
   Partner    W     E    You
   ◊ A J 6 4     S       ◊ K 10 2
              Declarer
              ◊ 9 7 5
```

If you play the ◊10, it will win the trick and the defenders can take the rest of the tricks in the suit. On the other hand, if you were to play the ◊K, the declarer would end up taking a trick with the dummy's ◊Q.

Playing the ◊10 in the above example is referred to as *taking a finesse against the dummy* since you are essentially doing exactly that – taking a finesse.

Many similar situations arise in third hand play and you will have to try to visualize the layout of the missing cards to decide exactly what to do. As a general principle, however, you want to keep the dummy's high card trapped whenever possible. By playing the ◊10 in the above layout, you are keeping your ◊K to trap the dummy's ◊Q. Here is a similar situation:

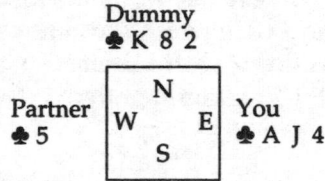

If the declarer plays a low club from the dummy on your partner's lead of the ♣5, you should finesse the ♣J, keeping your ♣A to trap the dummy's ♣K. The layout you are visualizing is something like this:

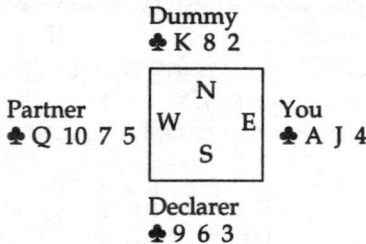

Playing the ♣A would give the declarer an unnecessary trick with the ♣K. What if the declarer rather than your partner held the ♣Q? For example:

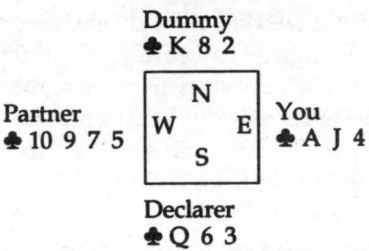

The declarer would win your ♣J with his ♣Q, but that is the only
trick he gets since the dummy's ♣K remains trapped. If you were
to play the ♣A on the first trick, the declarer would get tricks with
both the ♣K and ♣Q. This type of situation is similar to that on the
following hand. The auction proceeds:

North	East	South	West
(Dummy)	(You)	(Declarer)	(Partner)
1◊	1♡	1♠	Pass
3♠	Pass	4♠	Pass
Pass	Pass		

Your partner leads the ♡7, top of a doubleton in your suit and this
is the complete hand:

Contract: 4♠

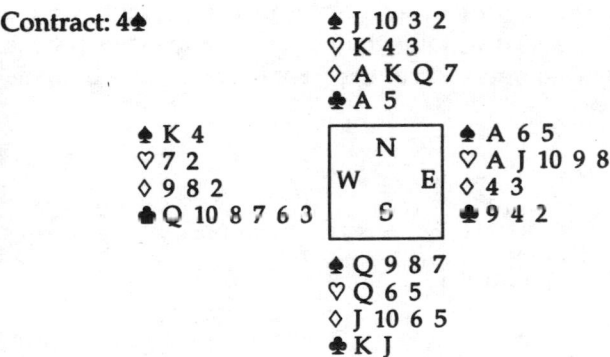

When the declarer plays a low heart from the dummy, your play
as third hand becomes critical to the success or failure of the
defence. If you win the trick with the ♡A, the declarer loses only
one heart trick and two trump tricks and makes the contract.

Instead, you must visualize the situation and insert the ♡8, taking a finesse against the dummy and forcing the declarer to win the first trick with the ♡Q. When your partner regains the lead with the ♠K, he can lead his remaining heart and the dummy's ♡K is trapped. Whatever the declarer plays, you win two heart tricks and end up defeating the contract.

Playing after your partner leads a high card

The same principles are used when your partner leads a high card, rather than a low card, and you have to decide what to do in third hand. The difference here is that your partner's high card may be high enough to win the trick. For example, your partner leads the ♠J against a no trumps contract and this is the layout you see:

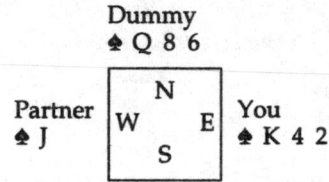

If the declarer plays a small spade from the dummy, there is no need to play the ♠K. Your partner's ♠J will be high enough to force out the ♠A if the declarer holds it, and will win the trick if he is leading the top of an interior sequence. For example, the complete layout might be:

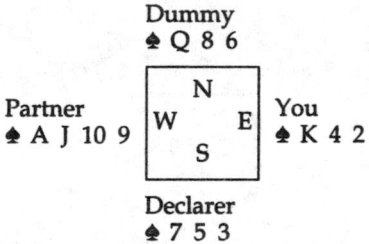

On the other hand, you will have to defend differently if your partner leads the ♠J and this is what you see:

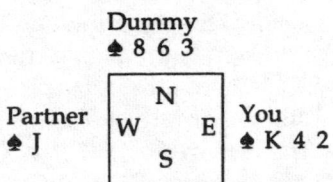

Your partner's lead of the ♠J tells you that he does not hold the ♠Q and, since it is not in the dummy, the declarer must have it. If you play a low spade, the declarer will be able to win the trick. Instead, you must play the ♠K on top of your partner's ♠J, visualizing the layout as something like this:

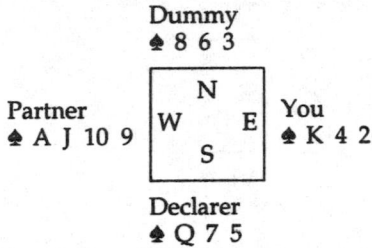

You can lead back another spade, trapping the declarer's ♠Q and taking all four tricks in the suit. What if the declarer, rather than your partner, holds the ♠A? After all, the complete layout might be something like this:

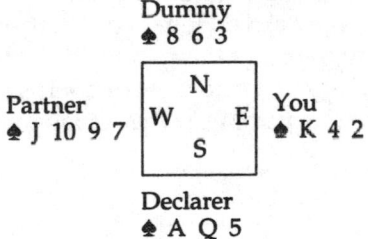

Playing the ♠K does no harm. The declarer was entitled to two tricks in the suit anyway.

You still follow the principle of keeping the dummy's high cards trapped whenever possible. For example:

Dummy
♡ K 8 4

Partner   N
♡ J   W   E   You
                     S   ♡ A 7 5 2

Although your partner's lead of the ♡J tells you that the declarer has the ♡Q, you should not play your ♡A when a small heart is played from the dummy. You want to keep the dummy's ♡K trapped if the layout is something like this:

Dummy
♡ K 8 4

Partner   N
♡ J 10 9 6   W   .   E   You
                         S   ♡ A 7 5 2

Declarer
♡ Q 3

Playing the ♡A would give the declarer two tricks in the suit.

Unblocking

We have looked earlier at the importance of playing the high card from the short side when the defenders are taking sure tricks or trying to promote high cards. Here is a situation in which you must be careful to do the right thing in third hand. Suppose your partner leads the ◊Q against a no trumps contract and the declarer plays the ◊A from the dummy in this situation:

Dummy
◊ A 6 4

Partner   N
◊ Q   W   E   You
                     S   ◊ K 5

You should *unblock the suit* by playing the ◊K on the dummy's ◊A! The situation you visualize is something like this:

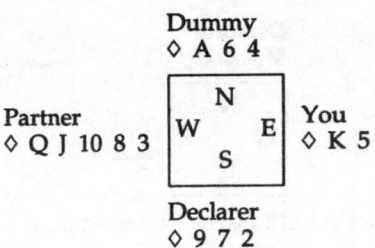

Dummy
◇ A 6 4

Partner
◇ Q J 10 8 3

You
◇ K 5

Declarer
◇ 9 7 2

If you hold on to the ◇K, you have no small card left to lead back to your partner's winners. You should play the ◇K even if the declarer plays a small diamond from the dummy on the first trick. That way, you can lead your ◇5 back to your partner's hand to help him promote the rest of his winners.

Returning your partner's suit

If you win the first trick and are planning to return your partner's suit, which of your remaining cards should you lead when you have a choice? In general, follow the same principle as when leading your partner's suit originally. That is:

- Lead the top of a doubleton (9 2, Q 3)
- Lead the top of touching high cards (Q J 8, J 10 9)
- Otherwise, lead low (Q 7 2, K 8 4 3)

In this case, we are talking about the lead you make from the remaining cards in your hand after you have played to the first trick. For example, suppose this is the situation:

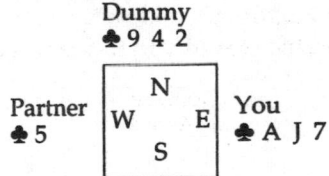

Dummy
♣ 9 4 2

Partner
♣ 5

You
♣ A J 7

Your partner leads the ♣5 and you play third hand high, winning the trick with the ♣A. Lead back the ♣J, top of your remaining doubleton. The complete layout might be something like this:

Dummy
♣ 9 4 2

Partner
♣ K 10 8 5 3

```
    N
 W     E
    S
```

You
♣ A J 7

Declarer
♣ Q 6

If you lead back the ♣7, rather than the ♣J, your partner will win the declarer's ♣Q with his ♣K and can lead the suit again back to your ♣J, but now his remaining winners are stranded. Returning the ♣J from your doubleton is following the principle of playing the high card from the short side to avoid blocking the suit.

Summary

When your partner leads to a trick and you are third to play, keep the principle of third hand high in mind. Only play as high a card as necessary to try to win the trick and, whenever possible, try to keep any high cards in the dummy trapped with your higher cards by finessing against the dummy.

When returning your partner's suit, lead back the same card from your remaining cards that you would if you were originally leading your partner's suit.

Over Zia's shoulder

Hand 1 Dealer: South

North	East (Zia)	South	West
		2NT	Pass
3NT	Pass	Pass	Pass

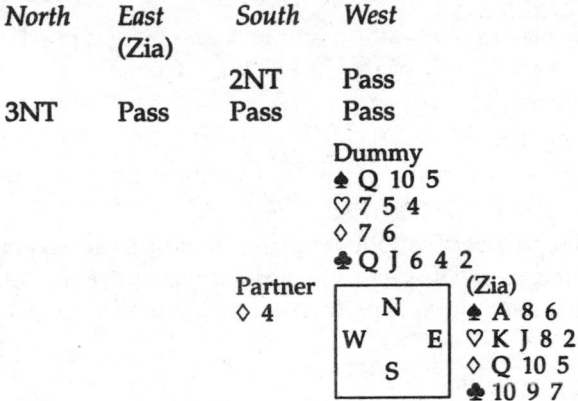

Dummy
♠ Q 10 5
♡ 7 5 4
◇ 7 6
♣ Q J 6 4 2

Partner
◇ 4

(Zia)
♠ A 8 6
♡ K J 8 2
◇ Q 10 5
♣ 10 9 7

Once again, South seems to hold most of the high cards. I have a few myself, however. How do I plan to put them to use after my partner's lead of ◇4?

Solution to Hand 1:

Contract: 3NT

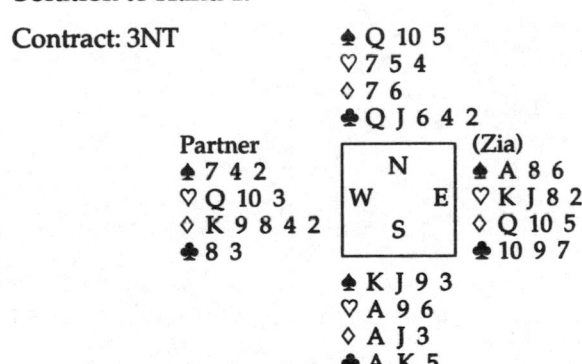

♠ Q 10 5
♡ 7 5 4
◇ 7 6
♣ Q J 6 4 2

Partner
♠ 7 4 2
♡ Q 10 3
◇ K 9 8 4 2
♣ 8 3

(Zia)
♠ A 8 6
♡ K J 8 2
◇ Q 10 5
♣ 10 9 7

♠ K J 9 3
♡ A 9 6
◇ A J 3
♣ A K 5

S We are going to have to come up with five tricks to put this contract down.

T The only sure trick we have is the ♠A.

O My partner has chosen the suit in which he wants to develop tricks and, with nothing clearly better in sight, it is up to me to help him out as best I can. It looks as though our plan is to try to establish diamond winners, using our high cards in other suits as entries.

P To help put the plan into operation we must start by playing the ◇Q, following the principle of third hand high. Our work is not done yet, however. The declarer takes the first trick with the ◇A, and then takes his five sure club tricks. When he eventually leads a spade, I must hop up with our ♠A and lead back my partner's suit. I return the ◇10, top of my remaining doubleton.

Had we played the ◇10 or ◇5 on the first trick, the declarer would win with the ◇J and have an easy time making the contract after driving out my ♠A. The principle of third hand high made our task easy on this hand.

Hand 2 Dealer: East

North	East (Zia)	South	West
	Pass	1♣	Pass
1◇	Pass	1NT	Pass
3NT	Pass	Pass	Pass

Dummy
♠ J 4 2
♡ A 7 6
◇ Q J 10 4 3
♣ A 2

Partner
♠ 6

```
      N
  W       E
      S
```

(Zia)
♠ K 10 7
♡ Q 10 9 8
◇ 2
♣ K Q 7 6 5

My partner leads the ♣6, the declarer plays dummy's ♣2 and I play ... ?

Solution to Hand 2:

Contract: 3NT

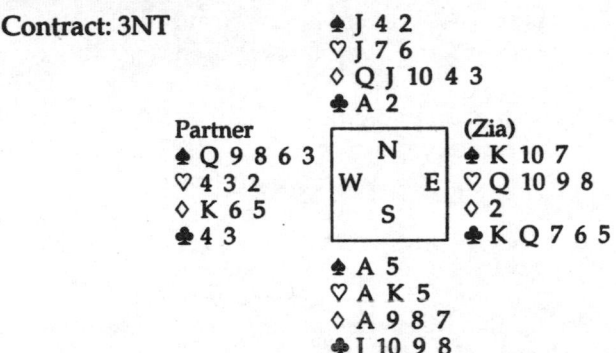

♠ J 4 2
♡ J 7 6
◊ Q J 10 4 3
♣ A 2

Partner
♠ Q 9 8 6 3
♡ 4 3 2
◊ K 6 5
♣ 4 3

(Zia)
♠ K 10 7
♡ Q 10 9 8
◊ 2
♣ K Q 7 6 5

♠ A 5
♡ A K 5
◊ A 9 8 7
♣ J 10 9 8

S We need to find five tricks to defeat the contract.

T In our hand, there do not appear to be any sure tricks.

O We might be able to establish tricks in hearts, if my partner has a high card, or in clubs by driving out the dummy's ♣A. But that is not our priority. My partner has chosen the suit to attack and I have no reason to doubt his judgement. Let's concern ourselves with helping my partner to establish tricks in the spade suit. I want to play third hand high, but only as high as necessary. Should I play the ♠K or ♠10 on the first trick? Relying on the principle of keeping the dummy's high cards trapped whenever possible, I should play the ♠10, keeping the ♠K to take care of the dummy's ♠J.

P Putting the plan into action, I insert the ♠10 and this drives out the declarer's ♠A. When the declarer tries an unsuccessful diamond finesse, my partner wins the ◊K and leads a spade to my ♠K. I lead a spade back to my partner's ♠Q and he takes two more spade tricks to defeat the contract.

Had we played the ♠K on the first trick, the defence would have had no chance. The declarer would win with the ♠A and drive out my partner's ◊K. The dummy's ♠J would prevent my partner from taking more than one spade trick and the declarer would make the contract. Thank goodness for those general principles of third hand play!

CHAPTER 11

Signals in Defence

Tennis champion Martina Navratilova says that when Wimbledon was rained out she spent her time playing bridge to keep her sharp and on her toes.

Each defender tries to form a mental picture of the unseen hands when making his plan to defeat the contract. The defenders have many opportunities to help each other throughout the hand. We have already seen examples of how the defenders can pass information through the card that they lead. Leading the top of a sequence, for example, gives your partner information about more than the actual card played. It tells him something about the next higher card and the next lower card. Playing the lower of touching cards when playing third hand high can also give him information, as we saw in Chapter 10.

When you are playing to a trick that you are not going to win, you sometimes have a choice of cards to play. The specific card you choose can be used as a *signal* to your partner to give him some useful information about your hand. In this chapter, we will look at how you can use such signals to tell your partner your attitude towards a suit, how many cards you have in a suit and what you would like him to do next. Of course, signalling is a two-sided affair. Not only will you have to give the appropriate signal when an opportunity arises but you will also have to watch for the signals he gives you during the hand, so that you can form a better picture of the hidden cards and amend your plan accordingly.

Giving an attitude signal

One of the most useful pieces of information you can give a partner is whether or not you would like him to lead, or continue leading, a particular suit when he has the opportunity. This is referred to as an *attitude signal*. The principle is quite simple: *a high card is an encouraging signal, a low card is a discouraging signal*. Let's look at an example where your partner has led the ♡3 against a no-trump contract:

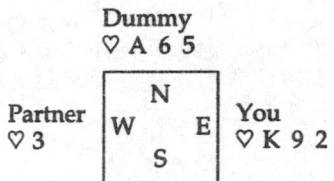

Dummy
♡ A 6 5

Partner
♡ 3

You
♡ K 9 2

If the declarer were to play a low heart from the dummy, you would have no choice about what to play. You would have to play the ♡K, third hand high, in order to win the trick for your side. If the declarer plays the dummy's ♡A on the first trick, however, you have a choice of cards to play. Since you like the suit your partner has led, you should play the ♡9, an encouraging card. If your partner regains the lead, he will know that you would like him to lead the suit again. Contrast the above layout with this one:

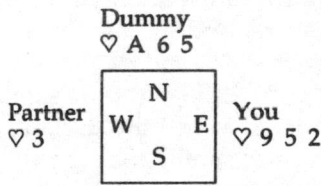

Dummy
♡ A 6 5

Partner
♡ 3

You
♡ 9 5 2

This time, you are not enamoured with your partner's lead so you would play the ♡2, a discouraging card, if the ♡A is played from the dummy. This will suggest to your partner that he find some other suit to lead at the next opportunity. Let's look at some examples in complete hands. On the first, the auction has gone:

North	East	South	West
(Dummy)	(Partner)	(Declarer)	(You)
	Pass	1♠	Pass
3♠	Pass	4♠	Pass
Pass	Pass		

Contract: 4♠

```
                         ♠ 8 7 4 2
                         ♡ J 9 7 6
                         ◇ A K 4
                         ♣ K 2
         You
         ♠ K 3          ┌─────────┐        ♠ A Q 6
         ♡ 10 8 5       │    N    │        ♡ 4 3 2
         ◇ J 10 9 3     │ W     E │        ◇ Q 8 5
         ♣ 9 8 7 6      │    S    │        ♣ Q J 10 3
                        └─────────┘
                         ♠ J 10 9 5
                         ♡ A K Q
                         ◇ 7 6 2
                         ♣ A 5 4
```

Against the declarer's 4♠ contract, you start off by leading the ◇J, top of your sequence, and the declarer wins the ◇K in dummy. The declarer then leads a small spade to his ♠J and you win with the ♠K. What do you do now?

Without the help of signals, this type of situation would be almost impossible for a defender. The opponents' auction has not given you much information and anything might be right. Your partner may have the ♡A and ♡K, and be hoping that you lead a heart, or he may have the ♣A and ♣Q and this is your last chance to trap the dummy's ♣K. Using attitude signals, however, makes the defence much easier. When the declarer wins the first trick with the ◇K, your partner should play the ◇8, an encouraging signal. Your partner, looking at the ◇Q, wants you to continue leading the suit to promote his ◇Q as a winner. If you have watched his signal, you will lead another diamond to defeat the contract. The defence ends up with a diamond trick and three spade tricks.

It does the declarer no good to try to discard his diamond loser on the dummy's extra heart winner before the trumps are drawn, since you will be able to ruff the dummy's ♡J. If you had not continued diamonds, however, the declarer would have been able to draw your small trump and then discard his diamond loser, making the contract.

You can sometimes use attitude signals to help get a ruff on defence. This time, we will put you in the East seat after the auction has gone:

North	East	South	West
(Dummy)	(You)	(Declarer)	(Partner)
		1♡	Pass
3♡	Pass	4♡	Pass
Pass	Pass		

Your partner starts off by leading the ♠A, top of his touching high cards and here is the complete hand:

Contract: 4♡

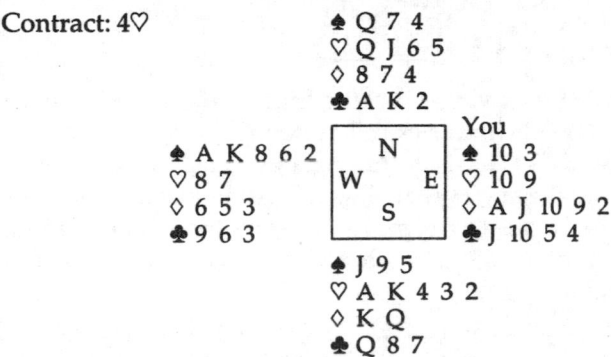

```
                    ♠ Q 7 4
                    ♡ Q J 6 5
                    ◊ 8 7 4
                    ♣ A K 2
                                    You
    ♠ A K 8 6 2      N         ♠ 10 3
    ♡ 8 7        W       E     ♡ 10 9
    ◊ 6 5 3          S         ◊ A J 10 9 2
    ♣ 9 6 3                    ♣ J 10 5 4
                    ♠ J 9 5
                    ♡ A K 4 3 2
                    ◊ K Q
                    ♣ Q 8 7
```

Which card do you play on the first trick? Again, this is an opportunity to use an attitude signal. Although you do not have a high card in the suit, you do have a shortness and would like your partner to continue leading the suit and give you a ruff. Your ◊A will then be enough to defeat the contract. To encourage your partner to continue, you must play the ♠10, not the ♠3. If you play the ♠3, a discouraging signal, your partner will not lead the suit again, being afraid to establish the ♠Q in the dummy as a winner.

Playing the ♠10 gives your partner the clue he needs about what to do next. He will realize that you must be encouraging him to continue leading the suit because you can trump the third round and so will continue by leading the ♠K and another spade.

You ruff this, take your ◊A and can now congratulate each other on your fine defence.

Let's look at one more example. This time, the auction goes:

North	East	South	West
(Dummy)	(Partner)	(Declarer)	(You)
1♠	Pass	2♡	Pass
3♡	Pass	Pass	Pass

                        ♠ A K 7 5 3
                        ♡ J 8 4
                        ◊ 8 7 2
                        ♣ A 3
        You   Partner
        ♠ 4 2   ┌─────────┐   ◊ 3
        ♡ K 9 7 3   │   N   │
        ◊ A K 5   │ W   E │
        ♣ J 9 4 2   │   S   │
                     └─────────┘

You lead the ◊A, top of your touching high cards, and your partner plays the ◊3 on the first trick. What now?

Your partner's ◊3 is a discouraging signal, asking you not to continue leading the suit. What should you do instead? Neither hearts nor spades looks too appealing, so you try leading a small club. You are amply rewarded when this turns out to be the full hand:

Contract: 3♡

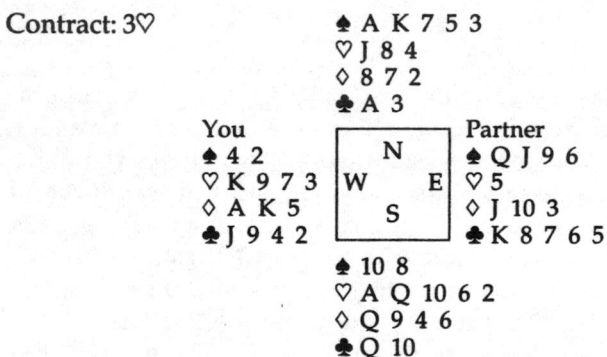

                        ♠ A K 7 5 3
                        ♡ J 8 4
                        ◊ 8 7 2
                        ♣ A 3
        You   Partner
        ♠ 4 2   ┌─────────┐   ♠ Q J 9 6
        ♡ K 9 7 3   │   N   │   ♡ 5
        ◊ A K 5   │ W   E │   ◊ J 10 3
        ♣ J 9 4 2   │   S   │   ♣ K 8 7 6 5
                     └─────────┘
                        ♠ 10 8
                        ♡ A Q 10 6 2
                        ◊ Q 9 4 6
                        ♣ Q 10

The club switch defeats the contract. When the declarer plays a low club from the dummy, your partner wins the trick with the

♣K and leads back the ♢J to trap the declarer's ♢Q. In addition to your three diamond tricks and club trick, you eventually get a trick with the ♡K. What if you had ignored your partner's signal and continued by leading the ♢K? You would have established the declarer's ♢Q as a trick and the declarer would make the contract.

Giving a count signal

Sometimes, it will be clear to your partner whether or not you like a suit. In these situations, it is usually more important to tell him how many cards you have in the suit. This is referred to as giving a *count signal*. The method for giving a count signal is quite simple: a high card followed by a low card shows an even number of cards; a low card followed by a high card shows an odd number of cards.

Of course, it is not quite so straightforward in practice. You need to recognize the situations that call for a count signal rather than an attitude signal. If you play a low card, your partner needs to know whether this is a discouraging signal or the start of a count signal. Also, you will not always have the luxury of being able to play two cards in the suit before your partner has to make a decision. He may have to assume that the high card you played on the first trick is the start of a signal to show an even number of cards, or that the low card you played on the first trick is to show an odd number of cards. In addition, you may want to start a low-high signal to show an odd number of cards but your lowest card is a seven or an eight. You will have to do the best you can with the cards you were dealt.

It is easier to see how a count signal can be put to use by looking at a complete hand. One common situation in which it is used is when the declarer is trying to establish a long suit in the dummy and has no entry outside the suit. Here is an example:

Contract: 3NT

```
                  ♠ 4 3 2
                  ♡ J 6 2
                  ◇ K Q J 10 6
                  ♣ Q 6
                                  You
  ♠ A J 9 7 6   ┌─ N ─┐    ♠ 8 5
  ♡ Q 7 5       │W   E│    ♡ 10 9 8 4
  ◇ 9 2         │  S  │    ◇ A 8 7
  ♣ 9 8 7       └─────┘    ♣ K J 10 5
                  ♠ K Q 10
                  ♡ A K 3
                  ◇ 5 4 3
                  ♣ A 4 3 2
```

The opponents reach 3NT and your partner leads the ♣7. The declarer wins the first trick with the ♣10 and goes about trying to promote the winners he needs to make the contract by leading a diamond. Look at what happens if you win the first or second diamond trick with the ◇A. When you lead back your partner's suit, the declarer plays the ♣Q and your partner wins the ♣A and drives out the declarer's ♣K to establish two more winners in the suit. But it does no good. On winning the ♣K, the declarer still has a diamond left to lead to the dummy's winners. He ends up taking two spade tricks, two heart tricks, four diamond tricks and a club trick to make the contract.

How could you have prevented this? Because the declarer started with three diamonds, you cannot afford to win the ◇A on the first or second round. You must wait until the third round. The dummy's diamond winners are now stranded. Try as he might, the declarer cannot get to them and he ends up with only two diamond tricks instead of four. This is called a *hold-up play* and the declarer often uses the same technique to try to strand the defenders' winners.

How are you to know that the declarer started with three diamonds? After all, if he only had two diamonds, you could win the second trick and the dummy's diamonds would be stranded. You could restrict the declarer to one trick in the suit. The answer, of course, is to make use of a count signal. When the declarer starts leading diamonds, it is obvious to both you and your partner that you are not interested in attitude towards the diamond suit – neither of you likes it. Instead, your partner can give a count signal by playing the ◊9 on the first trick and the ◊2 on the second trick, high-low to show an even number. Since the declarer has shown up with a couple of diamonds, you know that your partner has two, rather than four, and that leaves the declarer with exactly three. This lets you know that you must hold up your ◊A until the third round of the suit. Had your partner played low-high in diamonds, to show three, you would have been able to win the second diamond trick in the knowledge that the declarer started with only two diamonds.

Giving a suit preference signal

The third type of signal that the defenders can use is a *suit preference signal*. This arises when you want to tell your partner which of two suits you would prefer him to lead, while you are playing a card in a third suit. The opportunity for this type of signal does not arise very often. It is only used when you clearly do not want to give an attitude signal or a count signal and when your partner is going to have to decide between one of two suits.

When the situation does arise, the basic principle is the following: a low card shows preference for the lower-ranking suit. As you can see, the situation for a suit preference signal must be very clear. Otherwise your partner will interpret a low card as a discouraging card or the start of a low-high count signal, and a high card as an encouraging card or the start of a high-low count signal. Nonetheless, a suit preference signal can be very useful when the opportunity arises.

Here is an example of the use of a suit preference signal when giving your partner a ruff:

Contract: 2♡

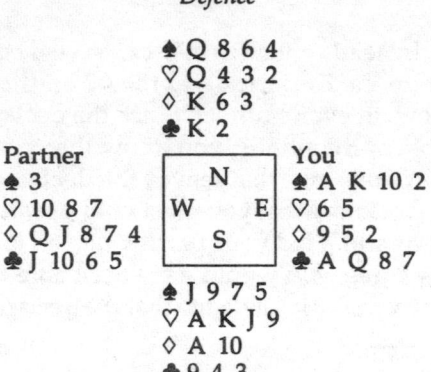

```
                    ♠ Q 8 6 4
                    ♡ Q 4 3 2
                    ◊ K 6 3
                    ♣ K 2
Partner                         You
♠ 3             N               ♠ A K 10 2
♡ 10 8 7    W       E           ♡ 6 5
◊ Q J 8 7 4     S               ◊ 9 5 2
♣ J 10 6 5                      ♣ A Q 8 7
                    ♠ J 9 7 5
                    ♡ A K J 9
                    ◊ A 10
                    ♣ 9 4 3
```

Against the opponents' partscore contract of 2♡, your partner decides to lead his singleton spade. You win the ♠K and ♠A and, when your partner shows out, lead another spade for him to ruff. So far so good, but what does your partner do next? Should he lead a diamond or a club? Without suit preference signals, he would have no way of knowing what to do. If he leads a diamond, the declarer wins, draws the remaining trumps and eventually loses two club tricks, just making the contract.

This is a hand where the suit preference signal can be put to use. After playing the ♠A and ♠K, you have a choice of leading the ♠10 or ♠2 for your partner to ruff. Since the spade you chose is clearly not useful as an attitude or count signal in the spade suit, it can be used to give a suit preference signal. Your partner is not going to be interested in leading back a heart, so his choice will be between diamonds and clubs. You would lead back the ♠2, your lowest spade, as a suit preference signal for the lower-ranking suit, clubs. When your partner ruffs this, he can use your signal to lead a club. The dummy's ♣K is trapped and you get two club tricks. You can then lead your remaining spade for your partner to ruff, defeating the contract. Had your clubs and diamonds been reversed, you would lead back the ♠10, your highest spade, as a suit preference signal for diamonds, the higher-ranking suit.

Summary

When a defender has a choice of cards to play in a suit, he can use the card he plays as a signal to his partner. The three types of signal he can give are:

- **Attitude signal** – a high card is an encouraging signal; a low card is a discouraging signal.
- **Count signal** – a high card followed by a low card shows an even number of cards; a low card followed by a high card shows an odd number of cards.
- **Suit preference signal** – a high card shows preference for a higher-ranking suit; a low card shows preference for a lower-ranking suit.

Both defenders need to be aware of what type of signal the situation calls for. In general, an attitude signal takes preference, followed by a count signal and then a suit preference signal.

Over Zia's shoulder

Hand 1 Dealer: South

North	East	South	West
			(Zia)
			1♡
2♢	Pass	2NT	Pass
3NT	Pass	Pass	Pass

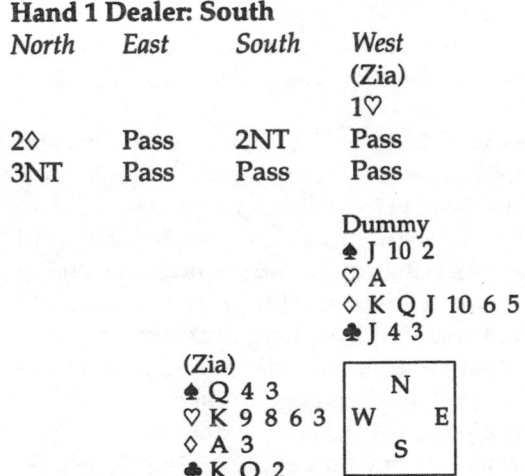

Dummy
♠ J 10 2
♡ A
♢ K Q J 10 6 5
♣ J 4 3

(Zia)
♠ Q 4 3
♡ K 9 8 6 3
♢ A 3
♣ K Q 2

Against the opponents' 3NT contract, I start with the ♡6, fourth highest of my long suit. The dummy's ♡A wins the trick as my partner plays the ♡10 and the declarer the ♡4. The declarer now goes about promoting some diamond winners by leading the ◊K, on which my partner plays the ◊9 and the declarer the ◊4. I hold up my ◊A on the first round, hoping to strand the dummy's diamond winners, but I have to take it on the next round as my partner follows suit with the ◊2 and the declarer with the ◊7. What do I do now?

Solution to Hand 1:

Contract 3NT

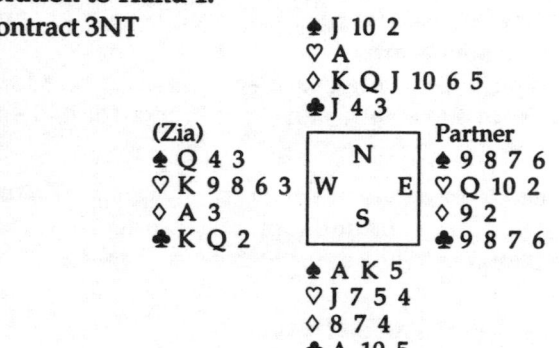

```
                    ♠ J 10 2
                    ♡ A
                    ◊ K Q J 10 6 5
                    ♣ J 4 3
  (Zia)                              Partner
  ♠ Q 4 3          ┌─────────┐      ♠ 9 8 7 6
  ♡ K 9 8 6 3      │    N    │      ♡ Q 10 2
  ◊ A 3          W │         │ E    ◊ 9 2
  ♣ K Q 2          │    S    │      ♣ 9 8 7 6
                   └─────────┘
                    ♠ A K 5
                    ♡ J 7 5 4
                    ◊ 8 7 4
                    ♣ A 10 5
```

S We need five tricks to defeat 3NT.

T Initially, we only have the ◊A as a sure trick but, once the dummy's ♡A is driven out, our ♡K has become a second sure trick.

O Needing three more tricks, I will have to hope that my partner has either the ♡Q or ♣A. It is too much to expect him to have enough high cards in spades to help defeat the contract. Before deciding whether to lead another heart of the ♣K, I should review what is happening with the diamond suit. I was hoping that the declarer had only a doubleton but my partner's high-low shows an even number so the declarer must have one left. I'll have to make the right decision on what to lead now, otherwise the declarer will probably manage to take at least nine tricks with all those diamond winners in the dummy.

My partner has given me the clue I need by playing the ♡10 on the first trick, an encouraging card. My best bet is to hope that he has the ♡Q.

P In putting our final plan into operation, I must be careful, at this point, to lead a low heart to my partner's ♡Q so that he can lead another one back to my ♡K. If I lead the ♡K first, the suit will become blocked when my partner wins the next trick with the ♡Q. There is no entry back to my hand.

As you see in the actual layout, leading a low heart after winning the ◊A is the only way to defeat the contract. It's nice to have a partner who knows how to signal!

Hand 2 Dealer: East

North	East (Zia)	South	West
	Pass	1♣	1♠
2◊	Pass	3NT	Pass
Pass	Pass		

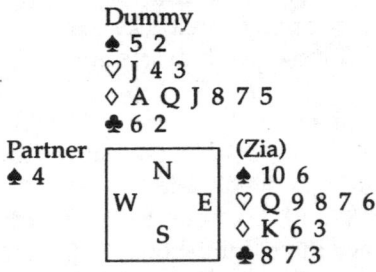

Dummy
♠ 5 2
♡ J 4 3
◊ A Q J 8 7 5
♣ 6 2

Partner
♠ 4

(Zia)
♠ 10 6
♡ Q 9 8 7 6
◊ K 6 3
♣ 8 7 3

My partner leads the ♠4 against the 3NT contract and I play the ♠10 on the first trick, third hand high. The declarer wins the trick with the ♠Q and plays the ◊10. My partner plays the ◊9 and the declarer plays a small diamond from the dummy. What do I do now?

Solution to Hand 2:

Contract 3NT

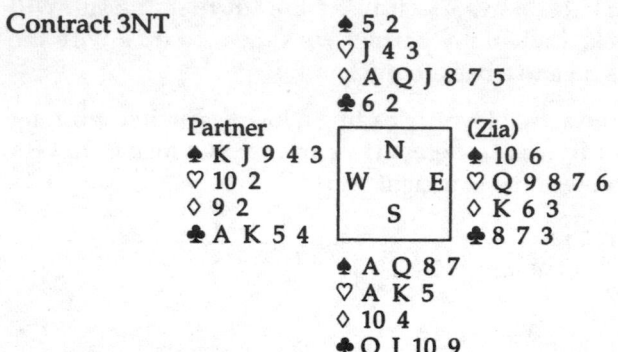

```
                               ♠ 5 2
                               ♡ J 4 3
                               ◊ A Q J 8 7 5
                               ♣ 6 2
        Partner                                (Zia)
        ♠ K J 9 4 3      ┌─────────┐         ♠ 10 6
        ♡ 10 2           │    N    │          ♡ Q 9 8 7 6
        ◊ 9 2          W │         │ E       ◊ K 6 3
        ♣ A K 5 4        │    S    │         ♣ 8 7 3
                         └─────────┘
                               ♠ A Q 8 7
                               ♡ A K 5
                               ◊ 10 4
                               ♣ Q J 10 9
```

S Once again we need five tricks.

T We don't start with any sure tricks but, when the declarer takes the diamond finesse, we have an opportunity to get one trick with the ◊K.

O My general plan is to help my partner establish his spade tricks and hope that he has an entry so that he can take them. It looks as if we should win the ◊K and lead another spade to drive out any remaining high cards in the declarer's hand, or perhaps trap a high card there. I must not be so busy planning to return my partner's suit that I ignore what the declarer is up to, however. The declarer is trying to establish the dummy's diamonds as winners. If we win this trick with the ◊K, he will be successful. My partner's ◊9 looks like the start of a high-low count signal to show an even number. If my partner has two diamonds, the declarer has only two diamonds and, by holding up our ◊K, we can strand the dummy's winners.

P We let the declarer win the trick with the ◊10 and there is nothing he can do. If he repeats the finesse, hoping my partner holds the ◊K, he will never get more than one diamond trick. If he switches to his club suit, he only ends up with two tricks in each suit, one too few.

CHAPTER 12

Thwarting the Declarer's Plan

Avoid detaching a card from your hand, ready to play, before it is your turn. This implies that you know what your opponents or partner intend to do before they do.

Although the defenders' objective is to develop the tricks they need to defeat the contract, they can also help themselves by preventing the declarer from taking the tricks he needs. We saw an example of this in the last chapter. By making use of the hold-up play, the defenders can sometimes strand some of the declarer's winners. Also, by holding on to the right cards when discarding, the defenders can prevent the declarer from taking an undeserved trick in a suit.

In this final chapter, we will take a look at other things the defenders can do to ensure that the declarer's tricks are kept to a minimum. We will concentrate on the defensive play by *second hand*. That is, when declarer leads a card from his hand or the dummy and you are next to play.

Playing second hand low

When you are the second player to a trick, there is not as much need for you to try to win the trick for your side. It is often to your advantage to wait and make the declarer commit himself first, since your partner will play last to the trick. For this reason, the common guideline for second-hand play is *second hand low*.

That is, when you have a choice of playing a high card to try to win the trick, or a low card to let the declarer or your partner win the trick, you should play the low card if you have nothing better to guide you.

Let's see why this is so. Look at the following layout of the heart suit:

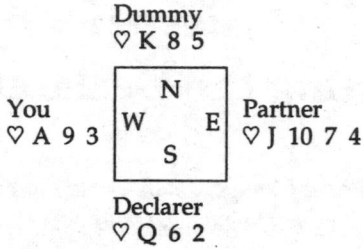

Suppose the declarer leads the ♡2 toward the dummy's ♡K. You can see that if you play a small heart, the dummy will win the trick with the ♡K. This might tempt you to play the ♡A. If you do, however, the declarer gets two tricks in the suit, one with the ♡K and one with his ♡Q. If you follow the guideline and play second hand low, letting the declarer win the first trick with the dummy's ♡K, that is the only trick he gets. The declarer's ♡Q remains trapped by your ♡A.

You should not always play low, of course. If you can see that taking your ♡A will certainly defeat the contract, then you should take it. It might be dangerous to play low and end up letting the declarer make the contract. Nonetheless, the guideline remains useful whenever you are uncertain what to do.

Here is an example in a complete hand:

Contract: 4♡

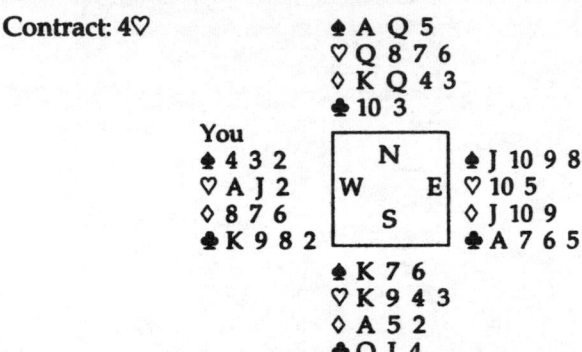

```
                    ♠ A Q 5
                    ♡ Q 8 7 6
                    ◊ K Q 4 3
                    ♣ 10 3
        You
        ♠ 4 3 2         N        ♠ J 10 9 8
        ♡ A J 2    W         E   ♡ 10 5
        ◊ 8 7 6         S        ◊ J 10 9
        ♣ K 9 8 2                ♣ A 7 6 5
                    ♠ K 7 6
                    ♡ K 9 4 3
                    ◊ A 5 2
                    ♣ Q J 4
```

You decide to make the aggressive lead of the ♣2, hoping that your partner will be able to help you in that suit. This works well when he wins the ♣A and returns a club to your ♣K for the second defensive trick. You now lead a spade, hoping to find that your partner has the ♠K, but the declarer wins the trick in his hand and starts to draw trumps by leading a small heart. There is no hurry to take your ♡A. You simply follow the principle of playing second hand low. The declarer has to play the dummy's ♡Q to win the trick, otherwise your partner would win the trick with the ♡10. When the declarer leads another heart, he finds that his ♡K is trapped by your ♡A and ♡J. Down he goes.

Keeping the declarer guessing

Apart from the technical merit of playing second hand low, there is another good reason behind the principle. The declarer often has to guess what to do and the more often you can make him guess, the more chance you have that he will go wrong. Look at this hand:

Contract: 4♡

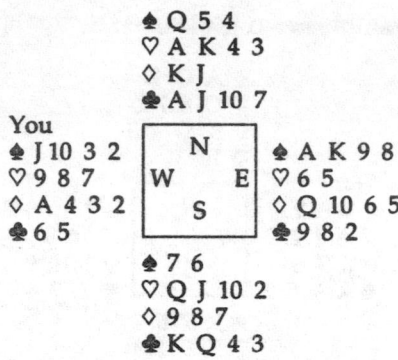

```
                    ♠ Q 5 4
                    ♡ A K 4 3
                    ◊ K J
                    ♣ A J 10 7
    You
    ♠ J 10 3 2      N           ♠ A K 9 8
    ♡ 9 8 7    W         E      ♡ 6 5
    ◊ A 4 3 2       S           ◊ Q 10 6 5
    ♣ 6 5                       ♣ 9 8 2
                    ♠ 7 6
                    ♡ Q J 10 2
                    ◊ 9 8 7
                    ♣ K Q 4 3
```

Against the 4♡ contract, you start off with the ♠J, top of your touching high cards. This works well when the dummy's ♠Q is trapped by your partner's ♠A and ♠K. Unfortunately, the declarer trumps the third round of the suit and proceeds to draw three rounds of trumps and then takes his four club tricks, ending up in his hand. Finally, he leads a small diamond towards the dummy and you ... ?

If you have been watching everything that has been going on, you should play a small diamond without any hesitation. When you play low, the declarer has to guess whether to play the dummy's ◊K or ◊J to make the contract. If he plays the ◊K, he makes the contract, since you have the ◊A, but if he plays the ◊J, he loses two diamond tricks.

If you play the ◊A, or even think a long time about whether or not to take it, you make the declarer's task easy. When you play a small diamond, the declarer may decide to play the dummy's ◊J, hoping that you have the ◊Q and that it is your partner who holds the ◊A. At least you have given the defence a 50-50 chance.

Covering an honour

One difficult decision that arises for a defender is when the declarer leads a high card, rather than a low card, from his hand or the dummy. If you hold a higher card, you have to decide whether to play it, *covering the honour*, or whether to follow the principle of second hand low. In such situations, there is a second guideline that says you should cover an honour with an honour if you are uncertain what to do.

Let's see where this rather contradictory piece of advice comes from. Suppose this is the layout of the diamond suit and the declarer leads the ◊J from the dummy:

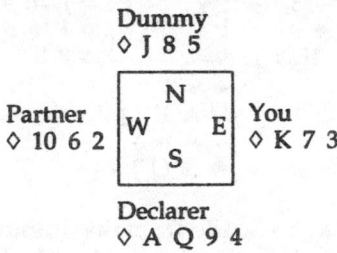

If you play second hand low, the dummy's ◊J will win the trick. The declarer can then lead another diamond from the dummy and your ◊K is trapped. Whether you play it now or not, the declarer ends up with all four tricks in the diamond suit. By following the principle of covering an honour with an honour, you can end up promoting a trick for your side. When the ◊J is led, you play the ◊K and force the declarer to win with the ◊A. The declarer can take a trick with the ◊Q, but now your partner's ◊10 has been promoted as a trick.

That is the idea of covering an honour with an honour. You hope to make the declarer use two of his high cards to capture one of yours and thereby end up promoting one or more tricks for your side. There is no point in covering an honour if you can see that there is nothing to promote for your side. For example, consider this hand where the auction has gone:

North	East	South	West
(Dummy)	(You)	(Declarer)	(Partner)
	Pass	2NT	Pass
3NT	Pass	Pass	Pass

Your partner leads the ♠5 and this is the complete hand:

Contract: 3NT

```
                    ♠ A 7 3
                    ♡ 6 2
                    ◇ Q J 10 8
                    ♣ 7 6 5 4
    Partner                         You
    ♠ K J 6 5 2     ┌─────────┐     ♠ Q 10 4
    ♡ 5 4 3         │    N    │     ♡ J 10 9 8
    ◇ 7 4        W  │       E │     ◇ K 6 5 3
    ♣ K 10 9        │    S    │     ♣ 8 3
                    └─────────┘
                    ♠ 9 8
                    ♡ A K Q 7
                    ◇ A 9 2
                    ♣ A Q J 2
```

The declarer plays a low spade from the dummy and you win the trick with the ♠Q and lead back the ♠10. The declarer plays low from the dummy again – the declarer also knows about the hold-up play – but has to win the ♠A on the third round. He now leads the dummy's ◇Q. Should you cover with the ◇K or not? Looking at all the high cards in the dummy's diamond suit, you can see that there is nothing to promote for your side by covering the ◇Q. You should play a low diamond. The declarer takes the finesse and leads the ◇J from the dummy. Again, you should play low. The declarer can win a trick with the ◇A, but only gets three tricks in the suit. He ends up with a spade trick, three heart tricks, three diamond tricks and a club trick. When your partner wins a trick with the ♣K, he takes his spade tricks to defeat the contract.

If you had covered either the ◇Q or ◇J, the declarer would capture your ◇K with the ◇A and end up taking four diamond tricks. Only cover an honour when there is the possibility of promoting a trick for your side.

Summary

As well as trying to take their own tricks, the defenders should look for ways to prevent the declarer from getting his tricks. In addition to making sure they hold on to the right cards during the hand, they can use tactics such as the hold-up play to strand the declarer's winners.

An important consideration in avoiding giving extra tricks to the declarer is second-hand play. In general, you should follow the guideline of playing second hand low when the declarer leads a small card from his hand or from the dummy. If the declarer leads a high card, you should cover an honour with an honour if there is the possibility of promoting a trick for your side. Otherwise, you should generally play low.

Over Zia's shoulder

Hand 1 Dealer: South

North	East	South	West
	(Zia)		
		2♣	Pass
2◊	Pass	2NT	Pass
3NT	Pass	Pass	Pass

```
                        Dummy
                        ♠ K 8 7
                        ♡ 9 4 3
                        ◊ 10 6 5
                        ♣ 8 6 4 2
            Partner  ┌──────────┐  (Zia)
            ♠ Q      │    N     │  ♠ 9 3
                     │  W   E   │  ♡ J 10 6
                     │    S     │  ◊ Q 9 8 7 4
                     └──────────┘  ♣ A J 3
```

South holds a big hand once again and North carries on to game with his meagre values. My partner leads the ♠Q and that wins the first trick. He continues with another spade but the declarer wins this with the dummy's ♠K. The declarer now leads a small club from the dummy. What should I do?

Solution to Hand 1:

Contract: 3NT

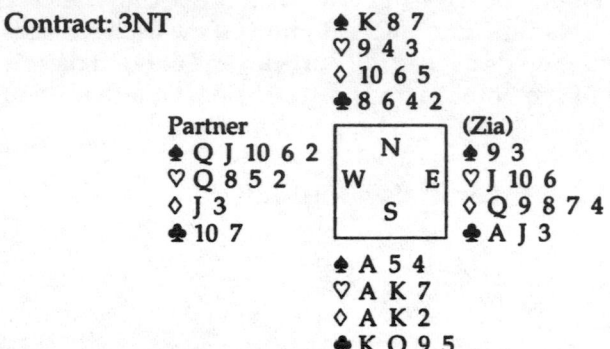

```
                    ♠ K 8 7
                    ♡ 9 4 3
                    ◊ 10 6 5
                    ♣ 8 6 4 2
Partner                              (Zia)
♠ Q J 10 6 2      ┌─────────┐       ♠ 9 3
♡ Q 8 5 2         │    N    │       ♡ J 10 6
◊ J 3          W  │       E │       ◊ Q 9 8 7 4
♣ 10 7            │    S    │       ♣ A J 3
                  └─────────┘
                    ♠ A 5 4
                    ♡ A K 7
                    ◊ A K 2
                    ♣ K Q 9 5
```

S We need five tricks to defeat 3NT.

T The only sure trick we have is the ◊A.

O It looks as though my partner knows what he is doing. He has led from a sequence and is trying to drive out the declarer's high cards to promote some winners. I'll have to hope he has an entry. When the declarer leads a club from the dummy, there is no need to panic and take my ♣A. I cannot see all the missing cards, so I should follow the general principle of playing second hand low.

P When I play the ♣3, the declarer wins the trick with the ♣Q. Unluckily for him, there is no other entry to the dummy which would enable him to lead towards his ♣K. He has to play a small club from his hand and hope that I started with a doubleton ♣A. When this is not the case, he ends up with the only two club tricks to go along with his two tricks in each of the other suits. That's only eight tricks.

If I had played the ♣A right away, I would have solved the declarer's problem of the lack of entries to the dummy. Playing low left him helpless. Notice that I couldn't afford the half measure of playing the ♣J. The declarer might win the ♣Q and lead the ♣K, felling my partner's ♣10 and promoting his ♣9 into a winner. If we are going to play low, we might as well play as low as possible.

Hand 2 Dealer: East

North	East	South	West
	(Zia)		
	Pass	1NT	Pass
3NT	Pass	Pass	Pass

Dummy
♠ A 5 2
♡ 7 4 3
◊ J 5
♣ A K 8 6 2

Partner
♡ 5

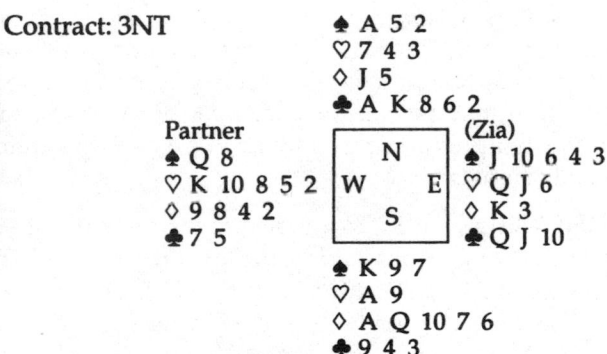

(Zia)
♠ J 10 6 4 3
♡ Q J 6
◊ K 3
♣ Q J 10

My partner leads the ♡5 against the 3NT contract and I play the ♡J, third hand high, but only as high as necessary. The declarer wins with the ♡A and plays a club to the dummy's ♣K. He then leads the ◊J from the dummy. Well, we have gone this far without letting the declarer make a contract. What do we have to do to defeat this one?

Solution to Hand 2:

Contract: 3NT

♠ A 5 2
♡ 7 4 3
◊ J 5
♣ A K 8 6 2

Partner
♠ Q 8
♡ K 10 8 5 2
◊ 9 8 4 2
♣ 7 5

(Zia)
♠ J 10 6 4 3
♡ Q J 6
◊ K 3
♣ Q J 10

♠ K 9 7
♡ A 9
◊ A Q 10 7 6
♣ 9 4 3

S Once more we need to find five tricks.

T As usual, we don't have any to start with. I guess we'll have to work hard to get them.

O My partner has led a heart and my ♡J has driven out the declarer's ♡A, so there is some hope that we are on the right track. In the meantime, we do not want to give anything away. The declarer's lead of the ◊J from the dummy presents us with a problem. Is it time for second hand low or should I cover an honour with an honour? Although I cannot see anything to promote, there is the possibility that I might promote a trick in my partner's hand by covering. After all, we will be getting two of the declarer's high cards for one of ours.

P I play the ◊K on the ◊J and the declarer wins the ◊A. He takes the ◊Q and ◊10, but now my partner's ◊9 is promoted into a winner. When the declarer forces out my partner's ◊9, he leads a small heart over to my ♡Q and I return one to defeat the contract.

It's a good thing I played the ♡J on the first trick to help my partner determine who had the ♡Q. I also did well to cover the ◊J. Otherwise, the declarer would get five diamond tricks and make the contract. Fancy my partner's lowly ◊9 being promoted into a winner. Oh well, I had to keep my record intact. I can't have my opponents thinking they can slip something by me when I'm on defence. It's too hard on my wallet ... and my ego!

Glossary

Attitude (signal)	A signal by a defender which tells his partner whether or not he likes a particular suit. A high card is an encouraging signal, a low card is a discouraging signal.
Broken sequence	A sequence in which you are missing the third card in a four-card or longer sequence.
Count (signal)	A signal by a defender which tells his partner how many cards he holds in a suit. A high card followed by a low card shows an even number of cards; a low card followed by a high card shows an odd number of cards.
Cover (an honour)	Play a card higher than the previous (high) card played to a trick.
Declarer	The player who first bid the denomination of the final contract. The declarer plays both his cards and the dummy's cards.
Defender	A member of the partnership which did not win the final contract. Both defenders co-operate to try to defeat the contract.
Divided	The way a suit is distributed between the two hands of a partnership. For example, five cards in the defenders' hands might be divided 3–2, 4–1, or 5–0.
Duck	To play a small card to a trick when you could play a higher card to try to win the trick.
Dummy	Declarer's partner. The dummy's hand is

	placed face up on the table with all the cards exposed and the declarer chooses the cards to be played from the dummy.
Entry	A high card, or trump, which allows the declarer, or the defenders, to get from one hand to another.
Finesse	An attempt to win a trick with a high card when a higher card is held by the opponents.
High card	One of the face cards – the ace, king, queen, or jack in a suit. (The ten is sometimes considered a high card.)
Hold-up play	Delay taking the winner(s) in a suit led by the opponents with the objective of making it difficult for the opponents to develop and take their winners in the suit.
Honour	The ace, king, queen, jack or ten in a suit.
Interior sequence	A sequence in which you have two or more touching cards and you also have a higher card in the suit.
Lose control	When the declarer has no trumps left and cannot prevent the opponents from taking all their winners.
Overtake	Play a card higher than the one already contributed by your side, even when the original card may win the trick.
Overtrump	Play a trump on a trick that is higher than one played previously.
Passive defence	Leading a suit which is unlikely to develop tricks for the defence but which is also unlikely to help the declarer make the contract.
Promote (winners)	Drive out the higher cards held by opponents in a suit in order to establish sure tricks for your side.
Repeat (finesse)	Take more than one finesse in a suit.
Return a partner's suit	Lead the same suit that a partner led when you have the opportunity.
Ruff	Play a trump when you have no cards left in the suit led.

Ruff and discard	Lead a suit in which both the declarer and the dummy are void while both still have trumps left. This allows the declarer to trump (ruff) in one hand and discard a loser from the other hand.
Second hand	The defender who has to play next when the declarer leads a card from his hand or the dummy.
Sequence	Series of touching high cards. For example the king, queen and jack in a suit make up a sequence.
Short suit	A suit of only one or two cards in a player's hand.
Show out	Discard when a suit is led.
Signal	Information given by one defender to his partner through the specific card he chooses to play in a suit.
Stranded	Winner(s) left in a hand to which there is no entry.
Suit preference (signal)	A signal by a defender which tells his partner which of two suits he would prefer led, while he is playing a card in a third suit. A high card shows preference for a higher-ranking suit; a low card shows preference for a lower-ranking suit.
Taking a finesse against the dummy	Playing a card other than your highest when your partner has led a low card and the declarer has not played the dummy's highest card. The objective is to try to keep the dummy's high card trapped by your higher card.
Third hand	The third person to play to a trick.
Trapped (card)	A card which can be captured by a higher card in the next opponent's hand when it is played.
Unblocking	Play the high card(s) in the short hand first so that the high cards in the opposite (long) hand can be promoted into winners.

| Uppercut | Tactic by a defender of trumping with a high trump in order to promote a trump trick in his partner's hand. |
| Winner | A card which will win a trick when it is played. |

Rubber Bridge Scoring Table

A rubber bridge score sheet is divided into two columns: We and They. There is a line across the middle of the score sheet, and points are scored both above and below this line.

Only points for tricks 'bid and made' are scored below the line. All other points are scored above the line.

You can score points in three ways:
- By making the contract your side has bid
- By defeating the contract the enemy have bid
- By earning a bonus score.

Score for bidding and making a contract

If you make a contract, the number of points you score depends on the denomination of the contract. For each trick above six, you receive:

20 points if the contract was in a minor suit (♣ or ♦)
30 points if the contract was in a major suit (♡ or ♠)
40 points for the first trick at no trumps
30 points for each trick after the first at no trumps.

Remember, only points for tricks bid and made are scored below the line. So, for making a contract of three hearts, you score 90 below the line. For making five diamonds, you score 100. For making six no trumps, you score 190.

A score of 100 points or more below the line is a *game*. You can achieve a game with a single contract (3NT, four of a major, five of a minor) or by making two or more *partscore* contracts which add up to 100 points or more. When one side makes a game, a line is drawn underneath the game score and any partscores already achieved by the other side no longer count towards game. A side which has made a game is said to be *vulnerable*, a side which has not yet made a game is *not vulnerable*. The first side to win two games wins the *rubber* and is given a bonus for so doing.

If you make more tricks than your contract, you score points for the extra tricks, but they are scored above the line. So, if you play in three hearts but make 11 tricks, you score 90 below the line and 60 above it. You have not made game – you do not have 100 points below the line.

Score for defeating the enemy contract

If you defeat the enemy contract, the points you score depend on whether the enemy are vulnerable and whether the contract was doubled or redoubled. If the contract was not doubled, you receive:

50 points for each undertrick if the enemy are not vulnerable.

100 points for each undertrick if the enemy are vulnerable.

So, if the enemy play in four hearts and make eight tricks, you score 100 points if they are not vulnerable and 200 points if they are. These points are then scored above the line.

If the contract was doubled, the scoring is:

Number of undertricks	Not vulnerable	Vulnerable
1	100	200
2	300	500
3	500	800
4	800	1100
5	1100	1400
6	1400	1700

and each extra undertrick scores a further 300 points. If the contract was redoubled, the score is twice the score for a doubled contract.

If you are doubled and make the contract, the score for tricks bid and made is doubled (and if this brings the total above 100, you make game – so two hearts doubled is a game contract because it would score 120 if made). If you make overtricks, you score 100 points per trick if not vulnerable and 200 points per trick if vulnerable regardless of the denomination. You also score a bonus of 50 points for making a doubled contract and 100 points for making a redoubled contract. So, if you played in two no trumps doubled and made ten tricks not vulnerable, you would score 140 below the line (70x2) and 250 above the line (100 for each overtrick plus the 50 bonus).

Bonus scores

You can earn bonus scores for bidding and making a slam contract as follows:

	Not vulnerable	Vulnerable
Small slam	500	750
Grand slam	1000	1500

The side that wins the rubber also scores a bonus of 700 points if the enemy has not made a game, or 500 points if the enemy has made a game.

Finally, you can score a bonus for holding what are called *honours*. If you hold in your hand alone four of the five highest cards in the trump suit – four of the A, K, Q, J and 10 – you score 100 for honours. If you hold all five, you score 150 for honours. If you hold all four aces at no trumps, you score 150 for honours. Declarer, dummy or either defender may score for honours. If you are declarer, you may claim your honours at any time, but if you are a defender you must wait till the end of the hand!

Index